THE SOUL OF A DEAL

RICHARD WOLPERT

Interviews include
J.J. Abrams
Andrew Braccia
Deepak Chopra
Maria Eitel
Reid Hoffman
Marc Geiger
Theresia Gouw
Peter Guber
Davis Guggenheim
Mellody Hobson
Joi Ito
Penn Jillette
Whitney Johnson
Larry Lessig
Amy Jo Martin
Jodie McLean
Dr. Dambisa Moyo
Tim O'Reilly
Michelle Peluso
Sean Rad
Mark Suster
Army Lieutenant Colonel
John Tien

ISBN: 978-1517657222

*I would like to dedicate this book to my two daughters
Grayson and Skyler, one of whom left this world far too young
and the other who brings me joy and pride every day.*

*A portion of all proceeds will go to the
Grayson R Wolpert Memorial Foundation.*

TABLE OF CONTENTS

PREFACE

I can hardly count the number of times a friend or a business colleague has said, "That definitely has to go in your book!" My response has always been, "What book?" to which they've rolled their eyes and said, "The book about your professional deals, of course!"

For many years, I questioned why anyone would want to read a book about my deals. Are my stories really that extraordinary compared to those of so many others who have had interesting and active careers?

During the last few years, I've worked primarily with young entrepreneurs just out of college. Reliving my stories through their eyes, I have come to realize that these may, in fact, be worthy and entertaining enough to put into a book.

I've had the opportunity to be a part of some high profile and historic events, and I've rubbed elbows with a number of industry leaders. I've sat across the negotiating table from both Steve Jobs and Bill Gates, and I've worked directly for several billionaires. But my life didn't start out that way.

I was born in Boston in 1962. My parents married as teenagers. My mother was 18, and my father was 17. They were both 23 when I was born. During the day, my father worked various hourly jobs to support his young family. At night, he went to Northeastern University to earn a degree in electrical engineering. We were poor. Barely able to make ends meet, we lived in a small two-bedroom apartment in a city slum.

When I was two years old, my father received his degree, secured a job at McDonnell Douglas, and moved our family to Los Angles. Even though he had landed a good job, my parents still struggled to get ahead. We lived in a series of different apartments around LA. It wasn't until I was 13, when my mother's father passed away and left them a small inheritance, that my parents were able to pull together enough money to buy their first home—a small but comfortable condominium in West Los Angeles.

Our condo was about a mile south of UCLA, where I went to college. My freshman girlfriend's brother and all of his friends were seniors, so we hung out with them a lot. I felt pretty cool chilling with a group of seniors. At the time, my major was undeclared, and I had no idea what to focus on.

At the end of freshman year, all of my senior buddies graduated. They had degrees in political science, history, and English, and none of them secured a well-paying job. One became a manager for a small sandwich shop; one worked for a caterer; one went to work for his father; one went to law school. This was a rude awakening for me. I knew that when I graduated, I wanted a prestigious job with a decent salary.

That summer, I studied the course catalog, reviewed all of the majors, and researched what types of jobs those majors would lead to upon graduation. After much consideration, I decided to take introductory courses in computer science, biology, and physics during the first semester of my sophomore year. Each of those subjects could lead to a nice job, so I figured whichever one I liked the best would become my major.

Taking those classes was eye-opening. Physics was the most intriguing and the class I did the best in. I received an A+ and was number one in my class, but there was something about computer science that felt more natural. The early introduction to programming using Basic, Cobol, and Fortran simply made sense to me and fit well with my innate thinking patterns. Soon, it became clear that computer science was the right major for me.

Once I decided on a major, the rest of my college career fell into place. I excelled in my computer programming classes. So much, in fact, that by my junior year, several professors had asked me to TA for them. This work was not only engaging, but it also paid quite well. Just as important, it gave me unlimited access to the computer lab, which was a valuable commodity. Most students had only a limited number of hours of access per week and were forced to code on big mainframe computers.

Then, in 1984, I was introduced to Macintosh. From that very first smiley face I saw on the screen to the startup sound that is still used today, I was an instant convert and believer. I was hooked on the massively advanced graphical user interface called WYSIWYG, which stood for "What You See Is What You Get." I had no doubt Macintosh was the future of personal computers, and I wanted to be a part of it.

I got ahold of an early-release, phonebook-sized manual and began writing simple programs for Macintosh. The computer was still so new, UCLA offered no courses on how to program for it. But my passion for Macintosh and its impact on personal computing continued through graduation.

After the post-graduation obligatory few-month trip to Europe, I moved up to Cupertino. I had no job and no prospects. But I bet that once I'd settled there, I'd find a contact at Apple. My bet paid off. Within just a few weeks, I met a relative of Apple co-founder Steve Wozniak, and I landed an interview. As someone who already knew how to write programs for Macintosh—there weren't many of us then—I was hired instantly and joined the software development team.

My programming foundation gave me an understanding of how computers work and how to make them do what you want—knowledge that has led to a varied and interesting career in the tech sector—but I'd always wanted to be an entrepreneur. In 1987, just a few years after I'd started at Apple, I launched my first startup, After Hours Software. For me, this marked a move away from computer programming toward a role as a business owner and manager.

In 1993, at the age of 31, I sold After Hours and spent a year integrating my company into Adobe. Then I took some hard-earned time off, much of which I was able to spend with my first daughter, Grayson. This time was special and I will be eternally thankful for it and cherish it, as Grayson passed away at the young age of 15, something I still struggle with every day.

During that year, I was pursued by Disney to be on the founding team of Disney Online, which was set to launch in 1995. Initially, I was senior vice president of technology, and then, at the age of 36, I was named president of Disney Online—one of the youngest-ever presidents at the company. I orchestrated Mickey Mouse's first-ever chat on the Internet and worked directly with Roy Disney on what Mickey could and couldn't say online.

I've invested in more than 50 companies and helped guide half of them to a successful acquisition or IPO, and I've started my own companies that have been acquired for millions. I've been invited to insider-only Grammy and Academy Award parties, and I've walked the paparazzi line as part of the "Diana Ross Entourage." I've taught classes at both Stanford and UCLA.

Upon resigning from my position as president of Disney Online, both Michael Eisner (then CEO of The Walt Disney Company) and Steve Jobs called to offer me jobs. I've attended a dozen weekend retreats with top leaders and executives from the entertainment industry, political world, and business sector. I've dined in the company of current and past United States presidents.

I've been tempted to join businesses that provide their teams with such luxuries as flying on private Gulfstream jets and cruising on mega-yachts. I've also been deposed in numerous legal battles, including the infamous Napster case, and I've been screwed by some very famous and powerful people (whose names I won't mention because I don't want to be screwed by them again).

Throughout all of these experiences, I've worked on hundreds of deals, from simple employment agreements to software distribution agreements, mergers and acquisitions, antitrust settlement agreements, key man agreements, and more. It's important to note that many of the deals I worked very hard on never came to fruition. As we'll discuss at various points in this book, being able to see signs of things going off track is *as important* as being able to see the next positive step in the deal process. Sometimes, you have to say "No." Not every deal should be consummated!

In most situations, I've been able to close the deal and over-index my peer group. I seem to be able to "feel" deals as they progress. The ability to know where a deal is in its lifecycle—and to nurture it or starve it as appropriate—is what has allowed me to close so many deals successfully.

Indeed, as I've closed more and more deals, I've realized that every deal has a "soul," and that my ability to understand this soul has given me an advantage. The soul of a deal is hard to define, but through my stories, it begins to take form.

This thread of deal making has been sown throughout my career. Sharing the soul of a deal is a good and useful way to tell my story, but more importantly, it's a way to educate others on how to get deals done. While this book may be most valuable for those in the business world, the ideas behind *The Soul of a Deal* are useful in everyday life and in the simple, routine exchanges we all have with others.

INTRODUCTION
DEFINING THE SOUL
OF A DEAL

C'MON, RICHARD. DO DEALS
REALLY HAVE A SOUL?

Absolutely. Just as human souls undertake a journey to find their way, deals follow a similar path. Deals, like life, have a beginning, a middle, and an end. Anything can happen along the way to keep a deal on track or derail it before it reaches the ultimate goal (consummation).

In understanding the checkpoints that come up during the life of a deal, you can learn to "feel the deal" and determine whether it is on track or off. This skill is paramount to understanding the soul of a deal. Catching a deal going off track as quickly as possible and getting it back on track just as quickly is the key to closing. If a deal stays off track for too long, it loses momentum. Its soul is starved, and it dies.

7

Throughout their lifespan, all deals develop characteristics that need to work in concert in order to keep the deals moving forward. However, deal making as I have experienced it is not as easy as following five to ten clear-cut negotiation steps. The purpose of this book is to illustrate how to identify a deal's unique qualities and challenges, learn as you go, and listen more than you speak in order to achieve the desired outcome. It is organized into the following sections to help guide and educate you as you work through your own deals:

1. When to Say "No"

   Not every deal should be done. Saying "no" now could lead to a "yes" later.

2. Understanding Personalities

   This is critical, especially if the parties involved have a history that could cloud a deal with what I call "historical residue."

3. Understanding Yourself

   What are you willing to give up to get a deal? This could encompass tangible items and/or abstract concepts related to your sense of self or ethics.

4. Taking Control of the Deal

   When is the right time to take very assertive action to control the deal process?

5. Pivoting Your Business

Certain deals can be instrumental in pivoting your business. Identifying these becomes particularly important when you realize the original vision for the business is its path to success.

6. Clever Assertiveness

    Distinct from directly taking control of a deal, clever assertiveness involves breaking logjams in a deft and non-threatening way to get the deal through.

7. Not Now

    Many deals that don't close initially may close in the future, when the right partners are at the table.

8. Sticking to Your Beliefs

    When you're faced with roadblocks or challenges that make you question your core beliefs, do not be deterred. Stick to your beliefs, even if it means a deal won't go through.

9. Fighting against a Much Larger Industry

    These are some of the hardest deals to get done. If you're a small fish negotiating in a massive pond, it can prove impossible to get a deal done on reasonable terms.

10. Being Young Enough to Take the Risk

    Youth and lack of experience—including having heard "no" infrequently or never at all—can embolden you to take risks you simply won't be willing to take later, when your career is more established.

This book contains two types of stories: narratives of my own deals and stories of others'. I've created the latter from interviews with an amazing and diverse set of people from a variety of fields including technology, entertainment, business, law, and politics. As these stories show, the core tenets of deal making apply across industries, and an understanding of the soul of any deal is critical to moving it forward.

My stories and those of my friends and colleagues will give you a better sense of how to "feel a deal" throughout its lifecycle. Your ability to negotiate and close deals will be much improved once you understand *The Soul of a Deal*.[1]

---

1   I started writing this book in May of 2014, WELL before Trump had publicly contemplated a run for president of the United States, let alone taken his seat in the Oval Office. Some people have asked whether this book is a counterpoint to Trump's *The Art of the Deal*, which was published in 1987. It is not. And if it were not for his presidency, I'm sure I would not be facing this or any other questions regarding the similarity between the title of my book and the title of his. Some people have warned Trump is litigious and may file suit against me, claiming that I purposefully titled my book to confuse readers into thinking it was his. Time will tell. In the meantime, I will say this: Despite the similarity between these books' titles, their structure, content, and insights are very, very different. I'm sure you will agree.

CHAPTER 1
WHEN TO SAY "NO"

SAYING "NO" TO STEVE JOBS

When I first got my executive job at Disney in 1996, I was hired as a senior vice president of technology. Even though I hadn't written code in several years, I still had a good grasp of how to work with and manage engineers and technical folks. We were preparing for the launch of Disney.com on the Internet. (Yes, before 1996, Disney.com was a blank screen.) I was also in charge of all of the desktop computers used by Disney Online and some of the company's other divisions.

My predecessor was a Steve Jobs fanatic and loved all things Steve, including the Next Computer. For those of you who are too young to remember, after Steve got kicked out of Apple in 1985, he founded a company called Next Computer. He hoped to dominate the consumer and business markets with his new leading-edge computer, the Next Cube. Unfortunately, the Next Cube had some of the flaws found in other Steve inventions. (Disclaimer: I love Jobs, but to be fair, I have to point these out.)

The two major flaws of the Next Computer were:

1. Its price. This was about $8,000, or roughly four times the price of a powerful PC.

2. Its closed operating system. This meant Next Computers were incompatible with any other type of computer system.

Within the first few months of my tenure at Disney Online, I recognized these flaws and set a new rule that *NO* new Next Computers were to be purchased. I required that anyone using a Next Computer switch to a Windows-based machine. I did not expect that my decision would resonate all the way up the chain at Next Computer—to Steve Jobs himself.

I soon found out that Steve was asking about the guy who didn't think Disney should be using the Next Computer. "Bring him to me!" Steve ordered, and soon after, I was summoned to Next so that he could share his vision with me and convince me to lift Disney's ban on his computers.

Let's not forget that my very first job after college was at Apple. It was the mid-80s then, and I'd seen Steve as a god. I'd had the utmost respect for him and believed he could do no wrong. By now, however, I'd matured a bit, and I could see the negatives of the Next's path. I didn't think Steve could persuade me to lift the ban on Next Computers. But I had to take the meeting. I mean, frickin' Steve Jobs was asking *me* to spend the afternoon with him! How could I refuse?

The meeting started simply enough in a nice conference room in Redwood City, California, where Next was headquartered. My Disney colleagues and I were escorted down to the cafeteria, where we ordered our lunch, and then we were sent back to the conference room to eat. After lunch, we were treated to a parade of Next executives who shared their vision of how Next Computer would become the de facto computer of the future.

As the day came to a close, the moment of truth finally arrived. Steve took me into his office for a one-on-one. I was quite nervous. I knew he was going to sell me hard, but I was confident that I would refuse to reverse my decision that Next was not a good platform for Disney. Going into the meeting, I was set against using Next Computers, and Steve had not done anything material to change my mind. He began, "Well Richard, I am sure that you now have a better understanding of the power of Next and our future vision. Can I count on you as one of our ongoing customers?"

Dressed in his characteristic uniform of tattered jeans and a black turtleneck, Steve leaned toward me and stared into my eyes so intently, I swore I could feel his eyes boring into me. All I was thinking was, *Wow. What a turnaround.* Here was Steve frickin' Jobs asking me if I would please be his customer.

This was probably one of the most difficult "no's" I have ever had to say, but I felt Steve deserved an honest answer. "Sorry Steve," I said. "I just don't think it makes sense for us to standardize on your computers. I believe we will have to continue our transition to Windows-based machines."

Steve appeared stunned. I don't think he was accustomed to hearing "no." Both his facial expression and his body language changed instantly. Simply by uttering "no," I had immediately become persona non grata. Steve seemed to lose interest in any further discussion. He told me that his assistant would see me out. Ouch. Naturally, I found his dismissal tough to handle.

You might think I was insane to say "no" to Steve Jobs. But then, you don't know the second half of the story.

Roughly a year later, by which time I had been promoted to president of Disney Online, we were releasing the first kids' online subscription service, Disney's Daily Blast. Blast was about a decade ahead of its time, given that the Internet was still so nascent. Most people were still using 28.8 modems. (If you're not familiar with the 28.8 modem or its predecessor, the 14.4 modem, let's just say they were about 1/100 the speed we have today.) We had dozens of people working on Blast, updating it every day with new online stories, daily jokes, interactive tchotchkes we called "DToys," and educational software.

Right around the same time, Apple purchased Next Computer. They brought Steve back to Apple as the interim CEO, or iCEO. (Steve preferred iCEO because it had the double wordplay of interim and Internet.) Soon after this, Steve announced Apple would be releasing a new breed of computer called iMac. It had a very distinctive design and would be available in five different colors—a first for the industry.

Even though I had turned Steve down when he was at Next, I was still a huge fan of his and a big Macintosh enthusiast. (My entire first company was built on the back of Macintosh.) I saw the iMac release as an opportunity to do a deal with Steve. Blast had been planned only for Windows. But if I could get Apple to help with the engineering, we could also release Blast for Apple computers—more specifically, for its new line of iMacs.

I shot Steve a note with the information about Blast and laid out the offer. I received an immediate response and an enthusiastic "*Yes!*" It is quite critical to understand that even though I had turned Steve down, I had done so with respect. Now, a year later, the opportunity to do a new deal had come up, and there were no hard feelings.

A few of the principles behind *The Soul of a Deal* were at play. One was that there was a mutual benefit: Steve got to say that a company like Disney was going out of its way to support the iMac, and Disney was able to release its product for the iMac, which had a strong foothold in the creative community. This deal also had momentum. We were on a deadline to ship Blast, and Steve was on a deadline to ship the iMac. These key factors converged and helped the deal proceed.

During the next few months, Apple sent us some prototype iMacs for development and testing purposes. (I still have one of the prototypes in my Macintosh collection today :-).) They also gave us effectively unlimited technical support to help us develop Blast for Macintosh.

And then came the piéce de résistance: Steve called one day and asked if I would accompany him on stage for his keynote address at MacWorld in New York, where he would present the iMac and announce that Blast would be available on it.

Accompanying Steve during one of his infamous MacWorld keynotes was truly a magical experience. He went through an overview of the iMac and then invited me on stage to demo Blast.

Needless to say, I had a blast ;-). (A video of this keynote is available on YouTube.[2])

It took several years and the ability to say "no" to a product Steve believed in, but eventually, we made a deal that benefited us both. That deal effectively fulfilled two desires and was supported by aligned goals and momentum. It was a win-win for both sides.

KEY POINTS IN THIS DEAL:

- The willingness to say "no" and walk away.

- Resistance to being persuaded by the other party's power or celebrity status.

- A demonstration of respect and a commitment to remaining on good terms whenever possible, including when a deal doesn't happen.

---

2   https://www.youtube.com/watch?v=gdYiqVzPjAc Tune to 1:08:00

J.J. ABRAMS

SAYING "NO" TO STEVEN SPIELBERG

I am fortunate enough to have gotten to know J.J. Abrams over the last ten years. In addition to being a creative force beyond compare, he is also a "mensch"—a Yiddish word that means "someone with high integrity and honor"—who devotes time to numerous philanthropic activities.

For those of you who have never had the pleasure of meeting J.J., allow me to do my best to describe him. In my opinion, the 51-year-old is his generation's Steven Spielberg and George Lucas rolled into one. Early in his career, J.J. sold three scripts: *Taking Care of Business*, which he wrote with Jill Mazursky, *Regarding Henry*, which starred Harrison Ford, and *Forever Young*, which starred Mel Gibson. This was an amazing start. J.J. then began to make his mark on television, creating and executive producing several successful shows including *Felicity*, *Alias*, and *Lost*. His talents run beyond even this: J.J. also composed the theme songs for all three of these shows, making him a true "triple threat."

I sat down with J.J. in his office at his production company, Bad Robot. The building's plain brick facade hides all the science fiction and playful imaginings inside. His office contains a comfortable sitting area near his desk and a wall of collectibles from various vintage TV shows and movies. When we sat down, the first story J.J. told me was about the time he said "no" to his idol and now mentor, Steven Spielberg.

The story goes like this:

With a handful of full-length feature films under his belt, J.J. was working on the third season of *Alias* and was in the process of preparing the pilot for his passion project, *Lost* with Damon Lindelof, when he was approached by Tom Cruise and Steven Spielberg. The pair offered him the job of writing the script for their upcoming movie, *War of the Worlds*. Needless to say, this was a huge meeting for J.J. Spielberg was his hero, and Tom Cruise was, well, Tom Cruise. Here they both were, asking J.J. to write a script for their movie. It was a huge opportunity. "If they come to you, the assumption is that you're going to do it," J.J. explained. "They don't come to you and expect you to say 'no.'"

J.J. recounted the details of the meeting. He told me he felt honored and privileged just to be in the room with Spielberg and Cruise. The three chatted about the possibilities for *War of the Worlds* for more than a few hours, and as they talked, J.J. was also able to share his vision for *Lost*. In our interview, J.J. recalled how Spielberg and Cruise graciously gave him feedback on the *Lost* project, even though they were essentially asking him to abandon it. They told J.J. to think about their offer, and he tried to figure out how he could take on both projects—the movie script for *War of the Worlds* and the pilot for *Lost* (in addition to subsequent episodes of the series in the event it was well received).

This was a huge struggle for J.J. There was Spielberg, asking him to write a script that Spielberg would direct. J.J. also had the chance to work with one of the biggest movie stars in the world. But *Lost* was his own creation. He was torn.

After a week of assessing the opportunities and drawbacks, J.J. decided on a simple answer: "No." If he tried to do both projects, he wouldn't do either one justice. His heart was more connected to *Lost*. Now, he needed to rack up the courage to tell his idol the truth.

He did. He called Spielberg and blurted out, "Thank you so much for this amazing opportunity, but I can't do this movie." When J.J. told me this story, he said he still remembers exactly where he was standing and what he was wearing when he made that call. The details of the memory are burned into his mind forever. He knew it was the right thing to do, but he couldn't believe he was turning Spielberg down. To his pleasant surprise, Spielberg was extremely gracious. Nevertheless, as J.J. recalled, he thought, "There goes my movie career!"

Unbeknownst to J.J., when Spielberg and Cruise left his office after their first meeting, his assistant had given Tom a "bag of swag" (a goody bag filled with products and tchotchkes) that included the first two seasons of *Alias*. A few months later, J.J. was in Hawaii shooting the last scene of the pilot for *Lost* when Cruise called him. Tom said he had just watched the two seasons of *Alias* and loved them, and he wanted to know if J.J. wanted to hang out.

Just a few weeks later, J.J. got the fateful call from Tom to direct MI3. (Even though Tom and J.J. had a budding friendship, the call actually came from J.J.'s agent.) This blew the young director's mind. First, he had an opportunity to direct his first feature film. Second, he was making a deal with a superstar he had turned down. J.J. later learned that Tom thought he had a good background for MI3 because of his work on *Alias*; they were both spy stories.

Since that time, J.J. has gone on to work closely with Tom Cruise on several projects. Steven Spielberg has also become a good friend.

This is another example of when "no" was not only the right answer, it also led to a future deal. As long as you maintain your stance with graciousness and humility, the integrity of the original opportunity remains.

KEY POINTS IN THIS DEAL:

- You must be willing to say "no" and walk away from a deal.

- If you are extremely passionate about a project and getting a deal done requires that you give that project up, stick with your deep gut feeling and say "no." J.J. clearly did this with *Lost*, and his decision was spot on.

CHAPTER 2
UNDERSTANDING PERSONALITIES

NO THANK, MICROSOFT, THAT
WILL BE $761,000,000

In 2005, I had worked for RealNetworks for roughly four years and had a lot of knowledge about the company. I knew its strengths and challenges, how to work with the key players and executives, and how to get stuff done. I had recently stepped away from my full-time role as the Seattle-based company's chief strategy officer in order to spend more time at home with my family in Los Angeles, but I continued to support the company's executive team, helping with deal making in my part-time role of executive strategic advisor. This was when this story of this chapter began to take shape.

A little background information: In 1995, RealNetworks pioneered audio streaming technology for the Internet, and in 1997, they pioneered video streaming technology for the Internet. All of this functionality was wrapped up in a nice product called Real-Player, which in the late 90s, became the #1 way consumers accessed streamed audio and video content.

Around the same time, Microsoft was deemed a monopoly by the U.S. government. (Federal authorities scrutinize potential monopolies to ensure they do not unfairly deter competition, which disrupts free markets and puts consumers at a disadvantage.) Nevertheless, the company wanted to get into the streaming media market. In 2000, they launched Windows Media Player to compete head-on with RealPlayer. At the time, most of the content available on the Internet was in RealPlayer's formats: RealAudio and RealVideo. As such, the release of Windows Media Player was met with several roadblocks, while RealPlayer continued to grow and enjoy widespread usage.

Then Microsoft started to play trick ball. Microsoft Windows was the #1 operating system, and 95% of PCs were Windows-based. All of the PC manufacturers (Dell, Compaq, HP, etc.) had to purchase or license Windows from Microsoft. Eventually, the company started offering manufacturers discounts if they agreed to install Windows Media Player on all of their machines, which would make it the default media player for streaming audio and video.

The manufacturers bit on the discount. How could they not? The operating system was one of their fixed cost items. Microsoft's plan started to work. The company seduced all the PC manufacturers into defaulting to Windows Media Player for audio and video streaming, and in the process, they significantly chipped away at the business RealNetworks had spent years developing. Microsoft even went so far as to preclude some PC makers from including RealPlayer on their machines! During the next few years, Windows Media Player took market share from RealPlayer, and Windows-based formats for digital audio and video became increasingly popular.

Were Microsoft's business practices unfair? Wasn't this a straightforward case of a company using its power as a monopoly to create unfair competition? Certainly, this was the position we took at Real-Networks, and as such, we filed an antitrust lawsuit against Microsoft in federal court.

We were hardly the only victims of Microsoft's behavior. Marc Andreessen had invented the first Internet browser, Mosaic, which later became known as Netscape. When Microsoft noticed Netscape's fast growth, it quickly began development of its own browser called Internet Explorer, or IE. Guess what? Microsoft went to computer manufacturers and told them they could get discounts on Windows OS licenses if they pre-installed IE and used it as the default browser. Netscape sued Microsoft, citing antitrust violations.

When we filed suit against Microsoft, the company was or had been involved in litigation with a series of companies, including Netscape/AOL, Sun Microsystems, and Novel. To settle its antitrust dispute with Netscape (now Netscape/AOL), Microsoft paid the company $750,000,000. This gave us a good indication of how much our case would be worth.

We resolved to protect our rights, and it was no small proposition. It meant a cadre of lawyers running up bills of nearly $1M/month. But what was our end game? If we won, did that mean PC manufacturers would no longer make Windows Media Player their default media player? And what if winning took five years? How long could we chase Microsoft down? We believed in our position and that the courts would rule in our favor, but we also realized that a win could come so far down the road that it would become a moot point. With these thoughts and variables in mind, we decided to explore the possibility of a settlement with Microsoft.

By this time, I was working part-time from my home in LA. My focus was on strategy and deal making. I had the full trust and respect of RealNetworks' Founder, Chairman, and CEO, Rob Glaser, who had worked for Bill Gates at Microsoft for close to ten years and left on less than perfect terms. Rob personally asked me to get involved in the Microsoft deal and lead the business negotiations. I was to work with our general counsel, Bob Kimball, who would handle the detailed legal issues.

Microsoft also put together a small team to negotiate the deal. They assigned Hank Vigil (a longtime Microsoft veteran and chief deal maker) as my counterpart, and Brad Smith, the general counsel of Microsoft, as Bob's counterpart.

At first, the teams' main focus was simply to try to get a sense of whether or not there was any possibility of a deal. Bob, Hank, Brad, and I had a few meetings. The chemistry was good, and we quickly developed a rapport and respect for each other. During the first few weeks of getting to know each other, our discussions were very broad. We all wanted to get a feel for what it would take for each side, under the right deal terms, to settle the case out of court.

After about a month of back and forth, it was time for someone to throw out a number. We had our marching orders from Rob, who didn't want to accept anything less than $1B. We weren't shy, so we went first. We presented our number. The Microsoft team immediately scoffed at us and said they were thinking in the $100M-$200M range.

All things considered, this was not a bad start. We all knew it would be a long and arduous negotiation. Now, at least, we knew what the bid and the ask were. Both teams signaled they were open to compromise—a core tenet of getting a deal done.

Then we got *the* call. Hank said that before we made any more progress on the deal, Bill Gates was requesting an in-person meeting. He wanted us all to look each other in the eye and make sure we were really on the same page. It was a straightforward request, so we agreed to do it. (*As if* we were we going to say "no" to Bill? Read on...)

We began discussing arrangements for the meeting. Where would it take place? Rob didn't want to do it at Microsoft, and Bill didn't want to do it at Real. Neither of them wanted to be seen in public with the other, so we agreed on a hotel in the middle of nowhere. The meeting would be held in a conference room on the first floor. Hank and I would text each other as we arrived to make sure our respective guys didn't walk through the lobby at the same time. The intensity of the negotiation over how and where to have the meeting should have signaled the deep tension that existed between Rob and Bill.

When the time came, the six of us met in a small conference room—Rob, Bill, Hank, Brad, Bob, and myself. We had agreed that we would NOT negotiate the deal in that meeting. The purpose was simply to allow Rob and Bill to check in with each other and "see the whites of the other's eyes" in order to determine whether we could move forward.

The meeting opened haltingly. Bill and Rob spoke in carefully worded sentences. Their history and current conflict were clearly at the forefront of their thoughts. Our auxiliary presence helped keep the conversation moving along, however, and as the meeting got going, the tension dissipated to a degree. Bill and Rob seemed to ease up quite a bit, but the two stayed away from discussing the deal itself. Their conversation was mostly about the state of the tech industry, its new developments, and how each was faring personally. Each of the men appeared to appreciate the other's perspective and intellect. The meeting lasted about an hour, which Bob and I thought was a good sign.

When the meeting ended, Rob and Bill left quickly. The remaining four of us stayed back and chatted for a few minutes. "How do you think it went?" we asked one another. We all thought it went pretty well, all things considered.

After this debrief, Bob and I drove back to downtown Seattle. We felt good about the meeting. We were some $800,000,000 off in dollar value, but we knew we were one step closer to doing a deal.

As Bob and I were talking, the phone rang. It was Hank. "I have some really bad news for you, Richard," he started. He explained that Bill felt a deal would not end the tension that had grown between Microsoft and RealNetworks over the years. Bill had long mistrusted Rob, and now he felt that Rob had not shown him enough respect during the meeting. The entire deal was off. There was nothing to negotiate.

I shared this information with Bob. We were both quite surprised. We thought the meeting had gone well, but we didn't account for the thickness of the historical *residue*—a shared negative past that at least one of the parties involved in a deal can hold onto—that still existed between Rob and Bill. Residue can kill any deal.

Rob and Bill had more of a complicated past than I had realized. Although Rob left Microsoft in 1994 on fairly reasonable terms, by

1997, things had gotten tense. Microsoft's anti-competitive behaviors led Rob to testify before Congress about the company's monopoly. Bill took personal offense to the testimony, making the relationship between the two men more strained and contentious. This *residue* overpowered our attempts to relieve the tension. It put our deal on ice.

No work or progress was made on the deal for the next three to four months. We continued to spend our $1M/month on attorneys, and Microsoft continued to defend their position, all the while achieving more and more market penetration with Windows Media Player.

In the meantime, the European Commission of the European Union was taking a very hard stance against Microsoft, citing the company's abuse of its dominant position in the market according to the EU's competition laws. The government's position was strengthened by some of Microsoft's troubles with AOL, Sun Microsystems, and RealNetworks, whose efforts in the EU were lead by Dave Stewart. Each of these cases provided valuable information the EU could use to build its own.

The pressure from the EU and the fact that RealNetworks was one of the contributing witnesses put us very much in Microsoft's face during this time. Microsoft began to see just how much damage U.S. companies could cause in the EU, especially given the details of Microsoft's tactics in the Netscape vs. Internet Explorer issue or the Window Media Player vs. RealPlayer issue. This gave us *leverage* to get a deal done. When used just right—meaning not too brashly or too aggressively—*leverage* can be a key factor in making a deal happen.

We sat patiently, believing we had a good case, and time went on. Meanwhile, Hank Vigil and I built a mutually respectful and trusted relationship. Each of us held a fair amount of sway on our respective teams. Our agreement to be straight with each other went a long way toward overcoming the residue between Bill and Rob. In the end, deals are done by people, not companies. The trust Hank and I built would prove to be key to getting this deal done.

After about five months of silence, I got a call from Hank. He believed a sufficient amount of time had passed for us to reengage. (Hank was using his well honed sense for the *soul of a deal*.) He said if we were open to it, Microsoft would participate in settlement conversations. I discussed this call with Rob, who said, "I'm open to it, but those bastards better pay us at least what they paid AOL ($750M), and not the ridiculous $100-$200M they offered before."

Hank and I made a pact: If we decided to move forward with the deal, we would not allow Rob and Bill back into the same room until the settlement agreement was signed. Letting the two of them get together in person or be too directly involved in the deal was certain to send our negotiations off course again. In fact, the four of us (Bob, Hank, Brad, and I) agreed on the steps necessary to get the deal done.

Right around this time, we added another person, Mike Slade, to our side of the deal. Mike was a valuable asset because many companies liked him, including (and especially) Microsoft. Mike's involvement helped to calm some of the negative feelings that were coming from Microsoft due to the historical residue.

During the next few weeks, we made some progress on price negotiations. Microsoft had paid Nortel $500M in a settlement. Feeling our deal was comparable, Microsoft said they were willing to come *all the way up* to $500M. However, Rob was still insistent on $1B. Given that we were making progress, he instructed us not to budge.

Talks stalled for the next month or so—long enough for Rob to be convinced that we were not going to get $1B. We were still spending $1M/month on attorneys, and the case seemed like it could go on for years. Rob told Bob, Mike, and me that as long as we could get over $750M, he would agree to the deal. We had made some great strides. But Microsoft was still at $500M, and as far as they knew, we were at $1B.

For weeks, things continued to move slowly. Yes, $750M was in the middle, but we were waiting to see who would blink first. It was high stakes poker involving sophisticated and experienced players. This defined the soul of this deal.

Hank called one morning and asked if we could have a conversation, just the two of us. I didn't realize this was the call that would get the deal done. Hank said the details of our conversation were not to be shared unless he and I agreed at a later time to share them. I concurred, and we got on the phone.

Hank laid out the issues: "Look, Richard," he said. "You're at $1B, and we're at $500M. The obvious move that neither of us has been willing to make is to go to $750M. Frankly, we would do $750M, but we won't offer it because we know that if we do, you guys will want to split the difference between $750M and $1B and ask for $875M. And Richard, we will NOT go to $875M. We paid AOL $750M, and we will pay you that same amount."

Hank was communicating with full disclosure. This spoke volumes about the trust he and I had built during nearly a year of negotiations. I told him he needed to do a little better than $750M so that we could end up with a better deal than AOL. He said, "Fine, we'll go to $760M, but that's final." I thought that was fair, but how would we get our teams to the same place and close this puppy? I asked Hank to give me some time.

I went back to my team, but I decided not to share the details of Hank's and my call just yet. I argued that it would be good if RealNetworks got at least what AOL did and said that if we could get $750M+, we should take the cash and run. We should stop spending the legal fees, I said. We should be free of this burden and move forward. Rob had already reached this point in his own thinking. We all agreed that we would do the deal for $750M+.

Next came another call with Hank. He and I discussed how things would work. I promised Hank that if he offered $760M, we would take it and not try to split the difference between $750M and $1B. Hank took me at my word, and we agreed to move forward with a group call involving both teams. This was a case where *trust built over time* made all the difference in the world. It was Hank's trust in me that led him to make that fateful phone call in the first place and that allowed him to throw out the $760M number.

On the next call with the lawyers and each of our teams (but without Rob or Bill), Hank laid out the situation. "Look, guys," he began. "We are at $500M, you are at $1B, and we haven't gotten anywhere in a long time. I am willing to put our best and final number on the table, but it is our best and final. There is no going up from there." Then, he offered $760M (by which Bob was amazed). We told Hank we needed to discuss the offer with our respective CEOs, and that we would get back to him and his team.

Later that day, Bob and I met with Rob. He was quite pleased that we had received such a high offer. He was even more pleased that it was slightly more than the AOL settlement. He said we could move forward with the deal, and that he would back it.

This was the beginning of what was an additional two-to-three-month process of drawing up a detailed settlement agreement. During that time, there was a little bump upward of $1M, which made the deal total $761M. After the amount was finally settled, all went pretty smoothly.

The only other hiccup came as the deal drew closer and closer to closing. Rob and Bill wanted to meet in person again to "look each other in the eye." Both deal teams honored our agreement that the two men would not meet in person until after the deal was signed; the meeting "just did not work out" for Rob and Bill until the morning *after* we had our finalized agreement in hand. When the meeting took place, Bill and Rob were able to look each other in the eye and touch base about what each would say during an upcoming press conference.

PostScript: During the month following the announcement of this deal, RealNetworks' stock jumped from $7 to about $12, an increase of roughly 70%. This deal was consummated only because of the trust that had developed during several months between the teams at RealNetworks and Microsoft. Sometimes, patience is key to achieving the best deal.

KEY POINTS IN THIS DEAL:

- When negotiating a deal where there is *residue* between the parties, you must understand the source of that history (good or bad) and use this knowledge to help you navigate the negotiations.

- You must be willing to walk away from a deal to get to the desired outcome.

- You have to know what your boss's *true* walk away position is. You also need to be able to negotiate to a minimum of that walk away position. This often requires treading along a fine tightrope of when and how much you share details of the state of a deal. This balancing act is something that can ONLY be learned from experience over time.

- If you can establish a trusted relationship with a key player on the other side of a deal—someone who carries some weight in the process and has the juice to make things happen—you'll be able to work together to overcome things that may otherwise kill it.

- Trust your instincts when disclosing what your side is willing to do to move a deal forward. This can be done only if you trust your counterpart to take your disclosure in good faith. Remember, the goal is to arrive at a mutually beneficial resolution, not just a new starting place from which to negotiate.

THE SCIENTIST AND THE RABBI

Many years ago, one of my best friends, Bill Putnam Jr., founded a pair of audio companies at the same time. One was called Universal Audio, and one was called Kind of Loud Technologies.

Universal Audio was a company Bill's father had originally founded decades before. (Milton "Bill" Putnam was a world famous recording engineer, having worked with Sinatra, Bing Crosby, and Nat King Cole, among others.) Bill re-founded the company with the stated mission of reproducing classic analog recording equipment in the tradition of his father and designing new digital recording instruments that incorporate the sound and spirit of vintage technology.[3] Bill's second company, Kind of Loud Technologies, was dedicated to building modern day software for surround sound production.

In the beginning, Bill had his hands full working out of the basement of his house as he got both companies off the ground. I became an investor in both companies immediately, even though some of the technology was beyond my scope of understanding. I believed in Bill 100% and was prepared to back him in anything he would do.

After the first year or so, the companies began generating revenue, and Bill took a small office space in Santa Cruz, California. For logistical reasons, he found a single space to house both Universal Audio and Kind of Loud. This enabled him to keep a close watch on both.

A few years later, surround sound production hadn't taken off as expected, and it became clear that the two companies' products

3   Source: UAudio.com, https://www.uaudio.com/about/.

were converging. Also, running them as separate entities had become inefficient. Universal Audio had come out with a hardware card that allowed users to do music audio processing directly on a computer, and Kind of Loud products were used as audio filters for that card. Bundles of Universal Audio products combined with Kind of Loud software were being sold everywhere.

Eventually, it became all too clear that Kind of Loud and Universal Audio needed to merge into a single entity—Universal Audio. However, the fact that the two companies had different ownership structures was a huge obstacle to this transaction.

Bill had separate sets of financial investors in each of his companies. Being a fair and reasonable guy, he came up with a formula according to which all of the investors in Kind of Loud would gain equity in the newly combined company. Bill compared the relative sales numbers of both companies, and given those numbers, he calculated a relative ownership that each of the two groups would claim in the combined entity.

This was a rational and fair approach to merging the two companies. The one hairball in the process was that one of the co-founders and partners of Kind of Loud, Thomas, had ownership in Kind of Loud but no ownership in Universal Audio.

Thomas was the prototypical hardcore engineer. He had obtained his PhD in Electrical Engineering from Stanford and was not very business-minded. On previous occasions, he had deferred to Bill on all of the business decisions for Kind of Loud. Now that Bill was trying to convert Thomas' equity in Kind of Loud into equity in the combined company, Thomas just didn't know how to deal with it. As Bill explained, "We pressed Thomas to work to figure this out. The line between the two companies was getting more and more blurred, and Universal Audio was really starting to take off, generating several million dollars a year in revenue."

Bill suggested that Thomas find someone who could help with the negotiations, and Thomas asked his uncle, who happened to be a rabbi, to step in. Thomas agreed to meet to discuss his equity so long as his uncle could accompany him and negotiate on his behalf. At the time, this request seemed reasonable enough, so we agreed. (And being a good Jewish boy myself, I figured having a rabbi present would do no harm.)

At this point, Bill had already set precedent for the relative values of the two companies by offering the investors in Kind of Loud shares in the combined Universal Audio. With the exception of Thomas, all of the investors with skin in the game had agreed to the proposal. Now, we needed Thomas to agree it was a fair deal.

I remember the day so well. Bill and I met at the office of Accel Partners, where I was a venture partner. We planned on walking the rabbi through the deal we had given all of the other Kind of Loud owners. We hoped he would see it was fair so that we could quickly put the deal to bed.

Then, the shit hit the fan. After we presented to the rabbi (who shall remain nameless out of respect for his privacy), he approached the whiteboard armed with a printout of a Wikipedia article and explained what *he* believed was fair. In a very animated way, which I hadn't expected from a rabbi, he argued that Thomas should own half of Kind of Loud, that Kind of Loud and Universal Audio were equally valuable (this was not the case), and that Thomas should own 25% of the combined companies. To put this demand in perspective, it amounted to roughly 5X of what we had initially proposed and the remaining investors had already accepted. Much to my surprise, the rabbi had turned out to be a "rogue"—and rogues kill deals.

This meeting went on for a few hours, and Thomas said nothing the entire time. He left the negotiations to the rabbi, and the rabbi went off the reservation.

Bill and I pleaded with the rabbi to calm down and take a more reasonable approach. He was yelling at us and accusing us of cheating Thomas, and we were not going to stand for it. Even with our pleading, the rabbi got more and more upset, and more and more demanding. He told us that he and Thomas had already conferred with an attorney and were prepared to file suit. The only solution he proposed was that we agree to his demand that Thomas get 25% of the combined entity, nothing less!

Reaching no conclusion, we called it a day. This was an example of the willingness to say "no": We accepted that we weren't going to reach an agreement and discontinued the meeting. I remember how drained Bill and I felt afterward. Trying to keep your cool in the face of someone being belligerent, threatening, and simply unreasonable always takes a toll, and that day, it certainly took one on us.

Over the next month, we made no progress on the deal. The only good news was that we could "feel" that the deal was simply not going to get done as long as the "rogue" rabbi was involved, so we spent little to no time on it. In emails, we reiterated our offer and said that while we thought it was in everyone's best interest to close the deal, we simply weren't willing to negotiate with the rabbi's unreasonable demands. Around this same time, Thomas decided he wanted to spend more time at Stanford and work on Kind of Loud stuff only occasionally.

As much as we could feel the deal was off the tracks, we knew it had to get done, so we worked on getting the rabbi out of the picture. Given that Thomas had taken a passive stance and made the rabbi his confidant, we had the brilliant idea of bringing in a "champion." Typically, a champion is an impartial third party who is trusted by both sides, has nothing to gain one way or the other, and can bring both parties to closure.

In this case, the champion came in the form of Albert Chu. Albert was a very successful technology executive and an investor in Kind of Loud. He was familiar with how we were bringing the companies together and had already signed off on the deal. Most important, Thomas trusted Albert. We were confident Albert could be the "champion" to get the deal to close.

We asked Albert to reach out to Thomas and propose that Albert step in and negotiate on Thomas' behalf. In return, Thomas would take the rabbi out of the picture. Thomas agreed, and we were off to the races.

Albert met with Thomas to get his perspective and thoughts on the deal. Albert also explained why he himself had taken the deal we had offered and why he thought it was fair. In the end, Albert was able to convince Thomas that the deal was fair, but Thomas requested that some of his equity to be purchased for cash so that he could live off that cash during his tenure at Stanford's audio lab.

Finally, we all came together for a meeting. Albert presented Thomas' demands, which he had shared with Bill and me beforehand. Bill and I were perfectly fine with Thomas taking some money off of the table, and in the course of the next hour, the four of us agreed on all material terms. Within a few weeks, we had everything drafted by the lawyers and signed.

Such is the danger of rogues and the power of champions!

Postscript: Universal Audio has gone on to become one of the top three companies in the professional audio space. Headquartered in Scotts Valley just outside of Santa Cruz, they have grown to 10X the size they were when this deal was consummated. They have grown organically, never having had to raise venture capital. Thomas spends most of his time at Stanford but still does some contract work for Universal Audio. I have no clue what has happened to the rabbi, nor do I care.

KEY POINTS IN THIS DEAL:

- Beware the *rogue* negotiator who doesn't understand the business, has an ulterior motive, and doesn't have enough at stake to close the deal reasonably.

- While I'm sure the rabbi thought he was helping Thomas with his hard-line approach, his desire to appear as a strong negotiator actually became a major impediment to getting the deal done. If a new person outside the company is brought in to "help" broker a deal, learn their agenda ASAP and adapt accordingly.

- Remember the cardinal rule: Be willing to say "no"! Once we accepted we weren't going to reach an agreement with the rabbi, we discontinued the meeting and opted out of any further discussions with him.

- This deal speaks to the importance of founder agreements. When a company is formed, you are entering into a several-year marriage, which will unquestionably be tested many times.

CHAPTER 3
UNDERSTANDING YOURSELF

DEEPAK CHOPRA

BEFORE A DEAL, I NEED TO DRINK MY TEA

Deepak is a force to be reckoned with. Originally trained as an endocrinologist, he became chief of staff at New England Memorial Hospital. However, in 1985, upon realizing that one's spiritual health is as important as one's physical health, he left traditional Western medicine behind. Since that time, Deepak has become a world-renowned author and speaker on spirituality and the mind-body connection.

In addition to running the Chopra Center for Wellbeing in La Costa, California, Deepak leads dozens of speaking engagements and workshops each year. He has written over 80 books, including 20 *New York Times* bestsellers. Apart from all of his accomplishments, one of the things that struck me about Deepak was his playful side.

He has made numerous cameo appearance in movies, some of which poke fun at him directly, and he often appears on late night talk shows wearing his now-famous rhinestone studded glasses.

I've had the pleasure of knowing Deepak for the last several years because I'm an investor in Intent.com, one of the companies his family founded. For this interview, Deepak and I met at his office in La Costa.

Like many of the other amazing people I have had the chance to interview, Deepak started off by saying he really didn't know how he could contribute to a book about deal making because he doesn't see himself as a person who does deals. However, as we began to discuss things, we both realized that he had done many deals, including numerous book contracts and a series of investment deals in technology-oriented companies in addition to negotiating with the La Costa Resort on where to base the Chopra Center. During our interview, it became clear that the process Deepak follows when deciding whether or not to do a deal is more relevant to *The Soul of a Deal* than any specific deal he has been involved in, though the stories of some of these hold their own intrigue.

As we dug into the conversation, Deepak told me his decision-making process was extremely influenced by Masura Ibuka, the co-founder of Sony. Deepak met Ibuka in 1995, just two years before he passed away at the age of 89. Deepak sought out the meeting because he wanted to better understand the process of a man who had achieved so much in terms of personal wealth and contributions to his country.

Deepak recounted the meeting in specific detail. Ibuka was already quite frail when they met, but Deepak could still sense his wisdom. He asked Ibuka what lessons he had learned throughout the course of such a successful career. And as if catering directly to Deepak's belief in the mind-body connection, Ibuka described his three-phase process for making important decisions.

> **Phase 1** involves gathering as many facts about the decision as possible. This requires intellectual rigor and an honest commitment to considering the objective facts about the deal in question and the parties involved. It also requires filtering out others' opinions and judgments.

> **Phase 2** involves letting the facts simmer (in other words, "sleeping on it") for as long as a week or more, depending on the complexity and importance of the decision.

> **Phase 3** involves sitting down alone with a cup of your favorite tea and sipping it slowly. For Ibuka, if the tea went down smoothly while considering his choices, he would move forward with the deal. If drinking the tea caused heartburn, he would pass on the opportunity.

Deepak told me that he adopted this same approach when it came to making decisions. At first, this approach struck me as too simplistic. But then, Deepak went on to explain it in more detail, relating it to his teachings on the mind-body connection. As Deepak described Phase 3, Ibuka's listening to his body through the ritual of drinking tea after processing facts was a way of connecting his mind and body. Deepak explained that the body always computes before the intellect because the body is "eavesdropping" on something bigger—the inner soul, if you will.

The body, Deepak went on to say, is more contextual, more relational, more holistic. After years of practicing Ibuka's three-step process, Deepak had come to trust the messages his body sent. If the body sent a message of comfort, he intuitively knew his decision would be okay. If the body did not feel comfortable, he trusted that, too. Deepak said that if he asks his body whether or not something is the right thing to do, his body will tell him. "My body is something that I trust now," he said.

According to Deepak, in order to trust your body, you need to be healthy. You have to sleep well, manage stress, meditate, and exercise. All of these practices transform your body into a "computer" that "listens" to what he calls the "cosmic computer." Deepak told me that listening to his body has become his "most trusted way to consider any deal or proposal." I thought to myself, "That's quite a process for someone who just told me he doesn't do deals!"

To understand the process in action, I pressed Deepak to tell me about the deal he had done with La Costa.

Deepak told me that when switched from being a doctor to his new career path, the last thing on his mind was "deals." His goal was to launch the new discipline of mind-body medicine, but he didn't have a lot of money.

Before he moved to La Costa, Deepak had run a center in La Jolla. His overhead, including the mortgage, was overwhelming. During this time, he happened to meet someone who knew the owners of La Costa. After meeting with them and hitting it off (and drinking his teas I presume :-)), he proposed, "If you give us a facility at nominal rent, we will promote La Costa and associate our brand exclusively with you. It will be a win-win situation for both of us." At first, La Costa was unconvinced. Then, they decided on a few-month trial period.

Deepak's passion for the mind-body discipline and his intuition about its power was so strong that he went $2 million in debt to launch the Chopra Center. He was so compelled by the vision and purpose of what he was doing, he felt he had no choice. It took years for him to pay off that debt. But pay it off he did. At the time of our interview, the Chopra Center had been in its current location for almost 12 years, and La Costa continued to take pride in the fact that they remained the center's exclusive landlords.

During our discussion, Deepak hit on a theme closely tied to the purpose of this book. Before doing a deal with someone, he first needs to understand their "soul profile," which essentially tells him what their real values are. To do this, Deepak asks a series of probing questions: What makes them happy? Do they have any peak experiences they treasure? What is their purpose? How are their relationships? Who are their heroes or heroines? What are their unique skills and talents?

Deepak also asks about the team they're working with. Does the team have a shared vision and purpose? Are they emotionally bonded? Do they complement each other's strengths?

By identifying a person's "soul profile" and observing whether their team is in sync with it, he can decide whether to move forward with a partnership or not. This is Deepak's own "soul of a deal" criteria.

KEY POINTS IN THIS DEAL:

- Tune into your intuition and let it guide you.

- Make sure you and the other party have an aligned vision.

AMY JO MARTIN

MAKING THE MOVE TO VEGAS
AT 30,000 FEET

Amy Jo Martin is a *New York Times* bestselling author and the founder and former CEO of Digital Royalty. She is also a pioneer in the fields of social media and celebrity.

Amy Jo began working in social media when she was employed by the Phoenix Suns. As she describes, she was one of the only people in the organization who knew anything about "new media" as it was known at the time, so they put her in charge of it. In 2008, when she was working with Shaquille O'Neal, Amy Jo began to have some of her early breakthroughs. Shaq was interested in connecting directly with his fans, and Amy Jo understood how social media could help him do this. The two had an informal working relationship that worked well for both of them. (Amy Jo thinks one of the reasons it worked so well was *because* it was an informal partnership. None of the usual players, such as managers or agents, was involved.)

One of Amy's first challenges with Shaq's project was getting people to believe it was actually *he* who was posting on social media. Amy Jo very cleverly came up with an idea called "Random Acts of Shaqness," where Shaq would stand on a street corner (he is hard to miss) and tweet out what he was doing. Others would chime in and confirm his identity and whereabouts. This was enough to convince the Twittersphere that Shaq was actually tweeting.

Amy Jo has a Twitter following of more than 1.1M herself, which she says is a result of getting in early and doing highly visible campaigns. People were still trying to understand social media at a time when she was doing some very groundbreaking things. She understood early on that in order to build an audience, you have to deliver value to the people who follow you.

Amy Jo was also one of the first to take the plunge into the Las Vegas Downtown Project headed up by Zappos CEO, Tony Hsieh. Tony, who had made a massive fortune by selling Zappos to Amazon, had a vision to create a technology community in the downtown area of Las Vegas appropriately named The Downtown Project. He began by purchasing a building for Zappos (part of the appeal of Vegas is that it has NO sales or income tax) and then purchased others nearby, many of which were run down and not in the "best part of town." Tony renovated these buildings and welcomed startup companies to come and join Project Downtown.[4]

I was curious what convinced Amy to get involved and move to Vegas, and she said it was a deal that was effectively consummated at 30,000 feet.

Amy Jo had met Tony several years before the launch of the Downtown Project. Around the time she first started on Twitter, she noticed Zappos was pretty active, so she direct messaged Tony to inquire about his social media policy. Much to her surprise, she received a prompt response. Tony said the Zappos social media policy was very simple: "Be real and use your best judgment." Through that initial connection, Amy and Tony became friends.

Years later, Amy Jo was flying around the country meeting with various investors about funding for her startup, Digital Royalty, but none of them felt right to her. On one flight, she messaged Tony

---

4   https://www.cnbc.com/2016/08/09/zappos-ceo-tony-hsieh-what-i-regret-about-pouring-350-million-into-las-vegas.html

about her startup, and he asked her to explain her vision. By the time she landed, the two had agreed on a valuation, and Tony had agreed to fund her company. He had also convinced her that she should move to Las Vegas and be part of the Downtown Project. They literally closed the deal via a high five in a Google Hangout. This was not your typical startup!

KEY POINT IN THIS DEAL:

- When something just feels right, don't second-guess yourself. Just go for it.

J.J. ABRAMS

SORRY, I DON'T THINK I CAN DO
THE NEW *STAR WARS* MOVIE

J.J. has had an amazing career and the good fortune to work with many extraordinary people. He has also amassed significant personal wealth in the process. His work schedule is intense, however, and one of its drawbacks is the negative effect on family life, which is especially pronounced when J.J. is shooting on location in a foreign country. In 2013, to help create and maintain the work-life balance he wanted, J.J. decided to take a six-month sabbatical to travel with his family.

Right before J.J.'s hiatus, Disney purchased Lucasfilm from George Lucas for $4B (a bargain IMHO) and began making plans to reboot the *Star Wars* franchise with a trilogy. Disney appointed one of their top producers, Kathy Kennedy, to put together the dream team that would create the new movies.

J.J. and Kathy had known each other for a long time, and Kathy knew that J.J. was her top pick to write and direct the first new *Star Wars* film. In late 2013, Kathy went to see J.J. at his Bad Robot office and made her pitch to have him come on board. As J.J. put it to me, "It was an incredibly, unbelievably, ridiculously, almost humorously tantalizing offer."

J.J. was flattered. But his response was a simple "No, thank you." Professionally, he had already been involved in two sequel reboot franchises (*Mission Impossible* and *Star Trek*), and he feared being pigeonholed as "that reboot franchise guy." He had also planned on taking that six-month break to travel with his family. Additionally, J.J. so loved the *Star Wars* movies he grew up on, he felt overwhelmed by the responsibility of taking over the franchise. There was a part of him that wanted to remain a *Star Wars* fan (instead of a creator) and see what someone else could do with the films.

Kathy's desire to have J.J. involved with the film did not waver, however, and she continued to pursue him. Eventually, she got J.J.'s attention when she explained that as a consequence of Disney's acquisition of Lucasfilm and its library, Disney and whomever they brought on to write and direct the new *Star Wars* episodes would have complete creative control and the ability to work from a blank slate. This information made the offer much more appealing. Michael Arndt was already on board as a writer, and Larry Kasdan was on board as a consultant. From that point, as the director, J.J. would be able to hire anyone he wanted to work with.

Kathy appealed to J.J.'s creative passion. She painted a picture of how J.J. could follow his own vision and make his unique mark on the *Star Wars* franchise. J.J. was nearly seduced by the offer but remained steadfast in his plan to take a six-month break with his family.

Finally, in one of their one-on-one meetings at Bad Robot, Kathy helped J.J. come to the realization that *Star Wars* was truly a once in a lifetime opportunity. This hadn't registered for J.J. at first, but once it became clear, he decided *Star Wars* was something he needed to do. Accepting the offer meant that J.J. could immediately get to work with a team he selected to make the movie he wanted to make.

J.J. told me *Star Wars* was one of the most exciting and fun projects he has ever had the opportunity to work on. Disney knew they wanted to incite a feeling with the audience, but they didn't have a story. They wanted a movie that was funny, mythical, moving, meaningful, colorful, and adventurous, and J.J. felt it was an ideal project for him. He believed he understood exactly what Disney wanted, and ultimately, the opportunity was impossible for him to resist. He decided to delay his family sabbatical, and for him, this was the right move. To put it in J.J.'s words, "It has been a dream scenario."

In the end, Kathy was able to convince J.J. to come on board by appealing to his passion. For J.J., passion was his primary motivator. It far outweighed other factors, including short-term financial gain.

Although it may sound trite coming from someone who has achieved a level of financial success, the reality is that if you ask anyone who has been offered an opportunity to pursue either their passion or short-term financial gain, you will almost always find that people who followed their passion feel they made the right choice. In fact, even J.J. had a story for me regarding a mistake he made when he chose money over passion.

Many years ago, J.J. was presented with the opportunity to write the screenplay for the reboot of the *Planet of the Apes* series. He was a huge fan of the series when he was a kid, and he was thrilled at the idea that he could write a new *Planet of the Apes* story himself. Around this same time, Jerry Bruckheimer offered J.J. a job that paid $50,000 more than the *Planet of the Apes* gig. It was relatively early in J.J.'s career, and $50,000 was a lot of money to him. Based on the higher price tag, J.J. went with the Bruckheimer project. To this day, this decision haunts him because he believes money was the wrong reason to have chosen the latter.

KEY POINT IN THIS DEAL:

- When we were wrapping up our interview, J.J. said, "When pressed with a decision where there is passion or more money... follow your passion every time."

CHAPTER 4
TAKING CONTROL
OF THE DEAL

PETER GUBER

I BOUGHT THE MOUNTAIN! AND FLYING IN TO PURCHASE THE GOLDEN STATE WARRIORS

Peter Guber is one of the few remaining media and sports moguls. In addition to running his entertainment and sports empire, Mandalay Entertainment, he is an actively involved co-owner of both the Los Angeles Dodgers and the Golden State Warriors. For many years, Peter was also the Chairman of Sony Pictures. Throughout his career, he has produced iconic films including *Batman*, *Flashdance*, *Soul Surfer*, and *Gorillas in the Mist*.

I met Peter about a decade ago, when we were both serving on the Board of Directors at the UCLA School of Theater, Film and Television, where Peter also teaches a variety of courses. At 72, he has more energy and charisma than most people I know in their 20s and 30s. In short, he is a force to be reckoned with.

My interview with Peter was fast-paced and filled with great examples of the soul of a deal. One of his more riveting anecdotes had to do with how he retained control over the 1988 movie *Gorillas in the Mist*.

Peter had a very strong desire to produce the film. He had been developing the movie in partnership with Warner Brothers and Terry Semel, and they felt they had a great script. However, people at the competing Universal Pictures wanted to make the same movie. On top of those two studios trying to control the fate of the movie, the talent firm CAA also wanted to produce it. Clearly, the movie had sparked a lot of interest and competition around who would make it and how.

Peter knew that multiple people could not make a movie about a woman and her relationships with gorillas. After all, it wasn't *King Kong*! Peter was fighting to get control of *Gorillas in the Mist*, but Michael Ovitz at CAA was sure he had it in the bag. Peter thought, "We're going to shoot this movie real. They're going to shoot this movie real. Who's the star of this movie? The gorillas. Where are the gorillas? On one little mountain peak in Rwanda."

As he was thinking this through, Peter had an epiphany and came up with a very non-traditional creative idea. He said, "Let's go over there and buy the filming rights to the mountain where the gorillas are. Let's make a deal with the government." Soon after, he and his partners flew to Rwanda and made a deal with the government whereby they retained the exclusive right to film on the mountain. Now, no one else could film the gorillas because they were on Peter's mountain. By securing exclusive filming rights, Peter had taken control of the movie.

As Peter explained, "My intuition was that the mountain was more important than even the script, the star, or the cast because the mountain had the one element that I felt was critical to making the movie. To create a successful film, we needed footage of the real gorillas with real actors. There was no CGI back then. It was just intuition. It sounded crazy, but that was the intuition I had." An intuition that worked amazingly well to his advantage.

A second interesting deal took place in 2010, when Peter and a team of investors he was working with made a successful bid to buy the Golden State Warriors. This was not the first time Peter had attempted to purchase a sports franchise; he had tried a few times before and been unsuccessful for various reasons.

Through the unsuccessful attempts, Peter realized acquiring a large sports franchise "is not a singular process. It was always a competition and a very, very aggressive and powerful one." Additionally, Peter explained, there are so many moving parts, you really never know where everyone stands until it all plays out.

In the Warriors deal, Peter said, he and his partner Joe Lacob were competing with "a lot of people—I mean A LOT of people" in an auction that was overseen by the team's then-owner, Chris Cohan. The auction put control of the bidding process in the hands of the seller and allowed him to drive the best price. During an early round, several people told Peter he would not win. Everyone predicted the victory would go to Larry Ellison from Oracle.

Peter and his partner knew they needed every possible advantage to win. Many of the other people they were up against were more powerful than they were. Joe Lacob suggested he and Peter call Chris and make a preemptive offer to buy the team. Then, the Thursday before the auction (which was scheduled for a Monday), Peter learned that Chris Cohan was on the East Coast, taking his son to see Duke University. Here again, Peter's intuition kicked in. He felt that making an offer in person would have much more of an impact and therefore a much higher likelihood of success. He suggested that Joe (who knew Chris) get on a plane immediately, fly to North Carolina, sit down with Chris over lunch, and explain the offer and why they were the best buyers. Peter thought Joe should tell Chris that if he liked the offer, he needed to accept it right then.

With the knowledge Peter had gained from all of the deals he had under his belt, he knew it was critical to get Joe and Chris in the same room for something this important. They needed to be face-to-face, breathing the same air. Peter also knew that although Chris wanted to maximize the price, owning a team was as much of a passion project as it was a financial one. Peter knew it would be a powerful play to look Chris in the eye and say, "If we win this bid, the benefits to you of our becoming the Warriors' new owners will extend far beyond the financial. We will protect the legacy of this team. We share your passion for the team, and we will continue to build and protect the legacy you created."

This strategy paid off. Joe and Peter's team became owners of the Golden State Warriors. In 2015, the team won the NBA Championship. (The Warriors went on to win again in 2017.)

During our interview, Peter was very generous with his time. He has great perspectives on deal making that merit being taken into account.

One is that the starting point of any deal is recognizing what it is that you desire to lend your commitment to. This desire translates into a passion more than a curiosity—the passion to acquire the project, the deal, the company, or the enterprise, and do whatever you want to with it. Without such passion, it is hard to drive through the formidable process of concluding a deal.

Another of Peter's perspectives is that the deal is the beginning of the beginning. It's not the end. If you're philosophically focused only on making the deal, you have the accent on the wrong syllable. You have to think past the joy of announcing of the acquisition. The deal is a means to an end that involves a long future of hard work.

This is why, Peter explained, when you initially embark on a deal, it's helpful to ask yourself a few questions and answer them honestly. "What's the compelling value proposition in obtaining it? Is it merely intellectual? Is it emotional? Is it beating somebody else out for it? Is it what I can do with it? Is it how I feel doing it?"

A third perspective Peter shared is that progressing from your initial desire to the closure of a deal requires a mix of three elements: an intellectual enterprise, an experiential enterprise, and an intuitive enterprise. Those three things carry you through the process. Sometimes, your intuition will push you to the point where your intellect says, "This not a good deal anymore." Sometimes, your passion and your desire will push you to take a greater risk.

But there are also risks if you are driven purely by passion ("deal fever"). Your passion can blind you to certain facts until it's too late—until the deal is closing, and the facts make the deal seem far less appealing. Remember: You don't have to make the deal until you make the deal. Facts are always revealed in the process. You'll learn about not only the seller's reputation, but also about their character and the characters of the other people involved. You'll also learn about the people you may have to deal with once the deal closes. During the deal-making process, you need to continually evaluate, "Is this good or is this not good?" You need to look at your own internal assumptions and ask, "Is this really what I thought it was?" More and more information is revealed with every step you take toward closing a deal.

A fourth insight Peter shared with me is that during the deal-making process, you have to be ambidextrous, and you have to be malleable. But drawing lines in the sand is also fine. By doing this, you are telling yourself, "This is as far as I want to go." You have to make sure you're following a clear principle. You also need to be clear about your core beliefs and values because if you deny your own beliefs, you'll end up having to question whether you've become lost in the process.

Deal making is a very organic process. It's different every time. There are a lot of moving parts in the equation of every deal, which means you have to learn how to understand each deal as its own distinct entity. Adding to this, the world is always changing. The economy is different each time, and your competition is constantly shifting. Don't let misleading factors such as "deal fever" overshadow your intuition.

KEY POINTS IN THIS DEAL:

- Sometimes, you have to be very creative and put yourself in a prime position by cutting a side deal in order to achieve your goal.

- In certain situations, negotiating in person is much more important and powerful than negotiating over the phone. Sometimes, you need to see the whites of the other person's eyes.

- Trust your intuition.

HOW STEVE JOBS HOODWINKED
THE MUSIC INDUSTRY

In the early 2000s, the digital music business was still trying to find its way. Label-backed services such as MusicNet and PressPlay offered poor user experiences and limited content, and they had few subscribers. Music subscription services such as Rhapsody had launched complicated platforms that consumers found difficult to use, and the platforms had seen only limited success. File-sharing services such as Kazaa (a successor of Napster) were doing very well on usage but generating no revenue. These services were also under siege—a barrage of music labels were suing them. On top of all of this, the total amount of revenue being created by the music industry was decreasing each year as consumers flocked to pirate sites and purchased fewer CDs.

Sellers of digital music needed a simple message. "Buy a song for $1" was floating around a lot at the time. Microtransactions were already becoming popular on the Internet. After all, who wouldn't be willing to pay $1 for a song they loved?

However, none of the music labels wanted in on the $1/song idea. They feared that unbundling albums and allowing consumers to purchase only the tracks they wanted would decimate album sales. Of course, what the labels did not realize was that, due to their inertia, they were *already* losing out on album sales. Thanks to services like Napster and Kazaa, consumers were developing the habit of spending *nothing at all* on digital music. Given this, even $1/song would be a win for labels.

Nobody could break the logjam until Steve Jobs made his play for Universal Music. Steve knew that if he could get Universal (the largest label at the time) to cut the $1/song deal with him, the other music labels would likely follow suit. They wouldn't want to miss out on something big.

Steve became chummy with Doug Morris and Jimmy Iovine, the two lead executives of Universal Music. Steve pointed out that Macintosh only had 5% market share of all personal computers and pitched Universal on allowing Apple to offer single tracks for $0.99. As Steve explained, the arrangement wouldn't really eat into Universal's market share, given that Apple's was so small. This logic almost persuaded Doug and Jimmy. But then came Steve's *piece de resistance*: He suggested that Apple was interested in buying Universal Music.

Over several months' time, Steve continued to have ongoing meetings with Jimmy and Doug to discuss the possibility of Apple either investing in Universal Music or buying it outright. Under the pretense that Macintosh had only 5% market share and the smokescreen of a potential investment in or purchase of Universal, Steve was finally able to convince Doug and Jimmy to give him the rights to sell their catalog for $0.99/track and $9.99/album.

To put this in perspective and to understand what a turnaround feat this was, the marketing that accompanied every ad for the iPod had been "Mix Rip Burn." Yup, you read that right: "rip" the music, then "mix" it, then "burn" it to your iPod. This had infuriated the music industry, as they felt Steve had been inviting people to "rip" off their music. But even with this history, the pair at Universal were so blinded by Steve's passion, celebrity, and the potential of selling their company that they went ahead and gave their catalog to Steve. In 2003, the iTunes Store was born. (As part of the deal, Doug and

Jimmy got Steve to stop using the Rip Mix Burn campaign, specifically the word, Rip.)

I was so shocked and frustrated that Steve was able to pull this off that I sent an anonymous flyer to the local press.

The Apple iTunes Music Store

How Apple profits from Music Piracy
With support and promotion
from the music labels

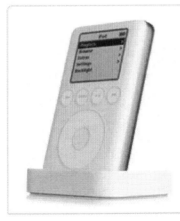

The all-new iPod
- New 20GB and 40GB models
- 10,000 songs in your pocket
- Works with Mac or PC
- Over a million sold

Now only $10,399.00

At the time, I was the chief strategy officer of RealNetworks and had led our $36M acquisition of Listen.com because I believed that subscription was the future of music in the digital age. From my vantage point, it was horribly frustrating to see the entire elite of the music industry become hypnotized by what came to be commonly referred to as the "Steve Jobs reality-distortion field." To me it was simple: Steve had a device he was selling for $200-$400 with a huge profit margin. The device was useless without music. All the labels needed to do was stand their ground and ask for a royalty for every iPod Apple sold.

If the music labels had had a vision for the future—or even an understanding of what was already happening to them—they could have turned iPod sales into a method of revenue generation for the entire music industry. This move likely would have reversed their fate. Instead, by cutting this "experimental" deal with Apple, the labels effectively ceded all power to Apple. They foolishly failed to ask for a percentage of the sales generated by the iPod—something that, IMHO, they would absolutely have been able to get at the time. This might have meant hundreds of millions of dollars of revenue. And yes, once Universal fell, all the other labels followed suit, looking very much like the lemmings in Apple's famous commercial from the late 80s.[5]

Once his deal with Universal was signed, Steve pulled a fast one on the music industry: He announced that the iTunes software (necessary to use the iPod) would be available for all Windows-based machines. In one fell swoop, he took a deal that was supposed to be an experiment for 5% of the industry and turned it into an Apple-controlled digital music empire for 100% of it.

---

5   https://www.youtube.com/watch?v=V-SJQdREDKM

Postscript: iTunes went on to become a digital store not only for music, but also for movies, TV shows, books, and more. After Steve cut the deal with Universal and launched the $0.99/track digital music offering, he discontinued conversations with Universal Music about Apple investing in or acquiring them. The iPhone, which came out a few years later, became one of the best and fastest-selling pieces of electronics in history. Much of the iPhone's success had to do with its vibrant content offerings from the iTunes store; however, 0% of the revenue (from the sale of the devices) went to anyone in the content business.

As I reviewed the framework for *The Soul of a Deal*, it struck me that one of the key factors that came into play in this particular deal was being blinded by celebrity. As successful and powerful as Doug Morris and Jimmy Iovine were, they got sucked into the "Steve Jobs reality-distortion field."

You have to hand it to Apple. They are one of the few companies that have managed to get music industry executives excited about legal digital music services. But Apple's real magic is that they have accomplished this even though their true business—and the only one they care about—has nothing to do with legal music and pays 0% revenue share to music labels.

During Apple's first month of operating the iTunes music store, the company heavily promoted the store's increasing popularity and was able to get the heads of most music labels to chime in on what a great success it was. The numbers Apple focused on—and the ones they convinced music label executives to focus on—were the number of songs sold from the iTunes store during its first month.

The numbers seemed impressive. But the question was, for whom? During that first month, Apple sold about 3M songs through the iTunes music store, and the music executives waxed poetic.

> "Hitting one million songs in less than a week was totally unexpected," said Roger Ames, Warner Music Group's chairman and CEO. "Apple has shown music fans, artists, and the music industry as a whole that there really is a successful and easy way of legally distributing music over the Internet."

> "Our internal measure of success was having the iTunes Music Store sell one million songs in the first month. To do this in one week is an over-the-top success," said Doug Morris, Universal Music Group's CEO. "Apple definitely got it right with the iTunes Music Store."

However, the real story—the one Apple was most focused on, and the one that was not beneficial to the music industry in any financial way—was how many iPods the company sold. While Apple sold an estimated $100M worth of iPods, $0 of this revenue went to the music industry.

But that's fair, isn't it? It's not like Apple leveraged the music labels or their most senior executives to hype and promote a device that was predominantly used for pirated music—a device that generates $0 for the labels. The music industry isn't *that* foolish. Or is it?

Industry estimates are that Apple pays the music labels approximately 70% of the money it collects for the sale of the $0.99 tracks. Every song in the Apple store is priced at $0.99. The iPods initially came in three models, 5MB, 15MB, and 30MB, which held about 1250, 3750, and 7500 songs respectively. So, if we were to assume that people were using these devices to support legal music they bought through the iTunes store, the fully loaded cost of the 30MB iPod with legal music from the iTunes store would be about $399 (the iPod) plus an additional $7,500 for a total of $7,899.

On top of this, Apple recently decided that the "iTunes store" was so successful that a 30MB iPod just wasn't big enough. As such, on September 8th, 2003, Apple announced it was discontinuing the 15GB and 30GB models, and replacing them with 20GB and 40GB models. As the slogan claimed, now you could have "10,000 songs in your pocket." As of this printing, the total cost of the premiere iPod—the one Apple makes most of its money from—would be $10,399.00 if it were filled with music from the iTunes store.

So what does all of this mean? Clearly, it means that the vast majority of songs stored on iPods—probably well in excess of 95%—are not songs from the iTunes store. And if those 10,000 songs are not from the iTunes store, where did they come from? Maybe people are sitting and "ripping" 1,000 CDs. But it's more likely that most of the songs on iPods came from some other "source." A source that also failed to yield any revenue to the music labels, such as Napster or Kazaa.

In the end, somehow, Apple was able to convince the music labels that promoting Apple and the iPod was a good idea, even if the device didn't generate any financial benefit for the music industry. And that, ladies and gentlemen, is magic!

KEY POINTS IN THIS DEAL:

- Sometimes, you can get a lot out of a potential partner by floating the possibility of a deal you never intend to consummate. (Note: I do *not like* this tactic, and I don't use it. I simply advise being on the lookout for it.)

- Sometimes, one party's celebrity and charisma can keep the party on the other side of a deal from seeing the bigger picture—so much so, in fact, that the second party misses out on the real opportunity and gives away the "keys to the kingdom."

- Often, people in non-digital industries underestimate how much their industry will be impacted by digital and Internet technology and business models.

TIM O'REILLY

SOMETIMES, THAT LAST
LITTLE BIT IS A BIG BIT

Tim O'Reilly has been a leader in the Internet space for more than 20 years. While I don't know him well (I was referred to him by my good friend, Joi Ito), Tim graciously agreed to let me interview him.

Tim is the founder of O'Reilly Media, which has been a prolific publisher of books and conferences in the Internet space. Additionally, Tim is a founding partner at O'Reilly AlphaTech Ventures (OATV). Among other things, he is credited with popularizing the terms "open source" and "web 2.0."

Tim started O'Reilly Media when he was just 24. He had never worked for anyone; he was a self-taught entrepreneur. From what he observed in the market, Tim started his company with the goal of not taking investment capital from a third party. During the past 35 years, he has grown his company organically and had an enormous impact on the industry through publishing, events, and technology advocacy.

The first story Tim shared with me comes from O'Reilly Media's early days, when it first became a publishing company. The company swiftly met with success, soon performing as well as any of the larger publishers. (O'Reilly would eventually outperform them in terms of average unit sales per title.) The usual suspects from traditional publishing began courting Tim, suggesting that he turn over product distribution to them. Tim asked how they could help grow his company and found their promises didn't hold up to due diligence.

Then Tim met someone he found refreshing: Günter Fuhrmeister, who was at Addison-Wesley at the time. Upon reviewing the financials of Tim's company, Günter told him, "You know, we really can't do much for you domestically. But have you thought about what we can do for you internationally?"

By taking a no-bullshit approach, Günter won Tim over. The two did an international distribution deal together, and later, after Günter had moved to Thompson International, Tim did a joint venture deal with that company. As Tim shared with me, "It was a testament to honesty and trust. When somebody's straight with you, it makes a lot of things possible."

KEY POINT IN THIS DEAL:

- Tim likes to quote Mark Twain, who reportedly once said, "Always tell the truth. You will gratify some people and astonish the rest."

Tim's second story centered on the time he sold GNN (the first web portal, which his company created in 1992). The web was still in its infancy, but O'Reilly was being pursued aggressively by venture capitalists who saw in GNN the kind of opportunity that smelled of big money. Tim wanted to keep his company private, so he didn't want to take venture capital. But he knew GNN couldn't succeed without outside capital, so he spun it out of O'Reilly and sold it instead. AOL purchased GNN in 1995.

As Tim explained it to me, the sale had to do with a book he had read that had left a strong impression on him.

The book was written by Bill Davidow, one of the original founders of Mohr Davidow, an early Silicon Valley venture firm. In the book, there was an appendix called the "Math of Market Domination." In that appendix, Bill wrote that in order to dominate a market, you need to own at least half the market and have the ability to grow faster than the market as a whole. Tim thought to himself, "Holy shit, the web is exploding. There's no way we're going to be able to keep up with the growth rate of the web without taking in capital. But I want O'Reilly to stay private." That's when Tim decided to spin out the project instead.

He negotiated the sale of GNN with David Cole, one of the heads of M&A for AOL. At one point in the negotiation, David offered both Tim and Dale Dougherty, the founder of GNN who was working for Tim, seats on what AOL was calling the Internet Advisory Council. Sitting on the Council came with stock options. However, as the deal for the purchase of GNN came to a close, David Cole took the Council appointments and accompanying stock options off the table. Tim refused to close the deal without them.

By contemporary standards, the deal was small (around $15M), and at the time, the paper value of each of Tim's and Dale's stock options was about $500K, representing a relatively small part of the overall package. The options turned out to be critical, however, because they proved to be one of the most valuable parts of the deal. In fact, they ended up being worth over $30M—more than 2X the negotiated price for the company the selling of which comprised the core transaction.

KEY POINT IN THIS DEAL:

- Don't overlook what may seem to be smaller parts of a deal, specifically parts related to the earnout of an M&A transaction. Those "bit" parts can often materially change the ultimate outcome of a deal.

PLAYING MUSIC TO THE BEAT OF
A DIFFERENT DRUMMER

When I was chief strategy officer at RealNetworks, we created a joint venture music service, MusicNet. After a year or so of running the business, we realized that a music service could survive only if it provided content from all five of the major music labels: Sony, Universal, EMI, Bertelsmann, and Warner Brothers. MusicNet had the backing of just three: Warner Music, EMI Music, and Bertelsmann Music.

While we had been setting up MusicNet, Universal and Sony had been setting up a competing service called PressPlay. As it played out (no pun intended), while we offered music from just three of the five major labels, PressPlay offered music from only the other two. Neither of us had a good platform.

Together, however, MusicNet and PressPlay could be perceived as having a duopoly, since the services were backed by all five major music labels. Other players could claim that, collectively, our two companies could limit competition and fix pricing, which would be an antitrust issue. This allegation was valid, and an enterprising young startup called Listen.com recognized this.

Identifying the risk this posed for music labels, Listen pitched all their new service to them. Their message was simple: "Give us a license to your music to avoid any antitrust issues, as we are just a small startup." This was a brilliant pitch, and in a relatively short timeframe, Listen leveraged it to become the first (and only) company with licenses to all five major labels. Part of the reason the labels were willing to license to Listen was that they didn't see this new startup with limited funding as a competitive threat.

At RealNetworks, we realized MusicNet's chances of survival were slim because it had access to only a fraction of the popular music available. In recognizing the enterprising accomplishment of Listen and its streaming service, Rhapsody, we decided that a better strategy than continuing to push MusicNet ourselves was to make a play for Rhapsody and buy Listen. There was one big hurdle: Listen's agreements with music labels gave the labels the right to approve or disapprove any acquisition that created a change of control (a new owner). If a label didn't approve, they had the right to terminate their content licensing agreement.

This put RealNetworks in a tricky situation. We were partners with EMI, Warner, and Bertelsmann on MusicNet. We were also the main company pushing and marketing MusicNet to the public, which was important to these labels. Internally, we decided we needed a more comprehensive product in order to have a compelling music offering. Since there was no way that Sony or Universal would ever license to MusicNet, the only way to get our comprehensive product was to buy Listen and offer Rhapsody. The question was: How would we get signoff from our label partners to allow us to keep the rights to all five major labels once we acquired Listen? Once again, the answer was to leverage labels' antitrust concerns.

We recognized that if we bought Listen and the labels refused to allow the licenses to stay with the Rhapsody product, the labels would likely be dinged for antitrust violations because there was no legitimate reason for them to say "no." As such, we went into 1:1 negotiations with each of the five major labels to get them to agree that they would continue to grant their rights to Rhapsody after we acquired Listen.

It took a few months, but ultimately, we were successful. We got all five labels to approve the acquisition before we made a formal bid to buy Listen. Once this was out of the way, we were free to pursue the purchase and acquire the Rhapsody product.

Our next step was to enter into negotiations with Listen's management team. Listen was a startup, and they had little brand recognition or money to market their product. They saw great value in having a partnership with someone like RealNetworks. Listen was also running low on cash, which gave the deal some momentum.

There is no one right method to negotiate a deal. With Listen, I decided we were going to stand our ground. We were going to come up with a fair and balanced offer, take it to the negotiating table, and hold firm at the number we came up with. This strategy was informed by some preliminary research.

By the time we were making our bid to purchase Listen, the company had raised about $30M. An overly simplistic note regarding venture investing and stock preferences: When a venture firm invests in a company, they get what's called a liquidation preference. In short, this means that when a company is sold, the investors with the preference get all of their money back first, and then the owners of the stock start to get their relative percentage.

In the case of Listen, this meant that if we paid $25M for the company, the investors would get all of it, while the management and employees would get nothing. Management wouldn't support the deal, and it wouldn't get done. We had to determine how much more than the $30M was fair and reasonable, given that the company was so new and had only tens of thousands of subscribers for its Rhapsody service.

We did some financial modeling, but most importantly, we simply asked ourselves: What is the maximum amount we are willing to pay for the business, given its potential? We believed we could sell hundreds of thousands of subscriptions. The number we came up with was $36M. We felt this was fair, given the company's progress and the value of its venture capital preferred stock, which we believed would be enough to motivate the management team to stick around and continue to run the business.

Our next step was to begin formal negotiations. We had Listen's senior management team fly up to the RealNetworks headquarters in Seattle for the better part of a day. Together, we went through our vision of the marketplace and how we believed RealNetworks and Listen would be more powerful together than apart (a typical 1+1=3 scenario). Listen agreed that it made good sense for the companies to come together.

At the end of the day, I told Sean Ryan, then the CEO of Listen, that we were prepared to pay $36M to acquire the company, and that we wanted to move forward. I went on to tell Sean that this was a post-negotiated number, meaning that this was our best offer, even though it was our first. I made it clear that Sean should either accept the deal or not—that this was the ending point of our negotiations.

Note: The "standing your ground" approach is one of my favorites. However, it's not always appropriate. You need to have a sense of the other side and know that they are motivated and/or under pressure to get the deal done quickly. This urgency creates momentum and knocks out a lot of bullshit, so in these cases, you can try the "stand your ground" approach.

A few days after the meeting in Seattle, Sean sent me a note saying Listen was interested in moving forward and that we should have a phone call to discuss next steps. Within days, we were on the phone. Sean wanted the acquisition to take place but came back with a number that was higher than $36M. Honestly, I don't even remember what his counteroffer was because I was simply not open to it. I'd meant what I said when I told him that $36M was our best offer, and I reiterated that.

Sean took the next week to test me on this. He went silent for a few days, which I let him do. Then, he sent an email saying how hard it was to get all of his different constituents to agree to a number. I told him I understood but offered nothing more. Again, Sean offered a compromise at a higher number. I said "no." We stood our ground, and finally, within a few weeks of our first meeting, Sean came back and said we had a deal at $36M.

The rest of the deal moved forward pretty rapidly, and all parties felt it was fair and balanced. The acquisition proved valuable for RealNetworks. Over the next few years (circa 2004-2009), Rhapsody became the leading music subscription service in the U.S. Its only real competition came from the newly formed Napster, which was effectively the PressPlay offering rebranded as Napster after the original Napster was shut down by federal authorities.

Postscript: Rhapsody is now a joint venture co-owned by Real-Networks and other investors. Rhapsody bought the Napster service from BestBuy, which had purchased it from Universal and Sony.

KEY POINTS IN THIS DEAL:

- In certain situations, you can leverage statutory laws—especially antitrust laws—to your advantage.

- If you understand the relative position of your negotiating counterpart and can determine whether time may be working against them, you can often negotiate a better deal.

- One powerful way to negotiate is to outline your best deal right out of the gate and stick to it. This approach takes tremendous discipline and a hard-line mentality. If your offer is fair, laying it out as your firm position up front can be a powerful and simple way to close a deal with little or no negotiation.

ARMY LIEUTENANT COLONEL JOHN TIEN

SOMETIMES, YOU HAVE TO TAKE OFF THE TERMINATOR OUTFIT

I have been fortunate enough to know John Tien for almost 20 years. John is a retired colonel from the U.S. Army who served several tours of duty in combat zones. He is a graduate of West Point and retired from the military in 2011. He now serves as an executive of Citibank. I am honored to call him my friend.

I wanted this book to cover a wide range of industries, and I found my interview with John particularly intriguing. Military and warfare strategy have long been the basis for theories of business strategy, beginning with such classics as Sun Tzu's *The Art of War*, written during the fifth century BC.

Like many of my friends, John was a concerned he didn't have any stories that were interesting enough for a book focused on the soul of a deal. And like those friends, he was wrong. John has countless stories involving strategy, risk, and feeling your way through the process of a deal, even when it goes 180 degrees against what you'd previously believed or had been trained to accomplish.

At the time of our interview in May 2015, ISIS had just made claims that they would seek out and attack members of the U.S. military and their families on U.S. soil. As a result, no troops with the exception of John will be named here, even though we owe them all our greatest gratitude for their service.

My interview with John focused on his tour of duty in the city of Tal Afar in the northwest portion of Iraq during the period of January to October 2006. His primary objective was to establish safety and security for both the troops on the ground and the citizens of Iraq. This was at a time when tension between the U.S. Armed forces and the insurgents in Iraq was at its most intense.

John and his group, which consisted of over 1,100 troops, began their training at The Combined Arms Training Center in in the small German city of Hohenfels. The Center had been a training ground for the U.S. military since the late 1950s, when the U.S. began defending West Germany against the Soviets. Up until 9/11, Hohenfels was the site of high-intensity combat training and war games for European-based U.S. troops

After 9/11, all of the training centers, including the one in Hohenfels, moved toward counterinsurgency training. U.S. troops still went to Hohenfels for tank and firearm training, but it was clear from Afghanistan and then from Iraq that counterinsurgency was the priority for the U.S. Army. Counterinsurgency is very different from traditional combat. It focuses on establishing security and stability for civilians and on training indigenous military forces rather than on the traditional "front-line" advances of World War I or II.

In preparation for the deployment in Iraq, the Army constructed a mock Iraqi city in the middle of the tree-lined hills of Hohenfels in order to prepare the troops for the conditions they would face. Their training included a two-week simulation during which they wore their full Army Combat Uniforms (ACU), including "interceptor body armor": an (IBA) flak vest loaded with ballistic protection plates, a Kevlar Helmet, a 9mm pistol, an M4 rifle, grenades, a Camelback water system, combat boots, Nomex fireproof gloves, and ballistic eyeglasses. As John described it, the additional sixty pounds of gear made him look and feel like something out of the Terminator movies.

The troops trained in the gear in Germany so that they would be prepared to wear it full-time in Iraq. The U.S. Army believed the Iraqis would trust in the strength of legions of combat gear-clad soldiers. John was also told to wear his uniform full-time during the simulation for his own protection. He also needed to be prepared to demonstrate that he was indeed the Terminator-capable force the Iraqis expected.

Balancing armed combat readiness with saving a village is complex at best and impossible at worst (if we are to view Vietnam as a failure). John and his troops needed to be prepared to deal with the anti-government of Iraq as well as Al-Qaeda-backed insurgents who did not want the U.S. to succeed in creating safety and stability. The enemy would disguise themselves as law-abiding and cooperative civilians to find ways to hurt or kill U.S. troops using snipers, roadside bombs, vehicle-borne bombs and—as the movie *Hurt Locker* made famous—"improvised explosive devices," better known as IEDs.

All of these factors made the simulated training in Hohenfels critical to John and his team's success on the ground in Iraq. All of the training needed to be executed under the presumption that everyone with whom they interacted in Iraq, including police and government officials, were insurgents.

John, as a lieutenant colonel, was the battalion commander. He was leader of the U.S. Army and Coalition force (NATO and The Coalition of the Willing, which former President George H.W. Bush had formed) charged with overseeing an entire Area of Operations

(AO) and an Iraqi city of 250,000 people. He had power, money, resources, and responsibility, and was the lead negotiator for all U.S. forces within his AO.

When they reached Tal Afar, John and his troops would encounter Iraqis from every walk of life: civilian women, people selling their wares, Iraqi police, Iraqi Army, and most notably, the local neighborhood leaders or sheikhs. It was with these sheikhs where John's "deal-making" abilities would be needed most. Throughout his two-week simulation, John was told that he had to negotiate with sheikhs who had different agendas, sometimes aligned with the U.S.'s and sometimes in direct opposition to it. His "deal" opposition would shift with every meeting.

The Army Scenario Masters gave John and his troops background information regarding how the sheikhs were viewed in the country and local neighborhood. Each of them wanted something different. Some wanted security, some wanted resources (money, improved civil services), and some simply wanted more power. In exchange, John wanted one thing: security and stability for the city and neighborhoods. He wanted peace.

In the simulation with the sheikhs, John was instructed to find his BATNA, which stands for the Best Alternative to Negotiated Agreement. While this is a common term in negotiation training, for Army lieutenant colonels formally trained to lead battalions of soldiers mounted on M1A1 Abrams Tanks and armed to the teeth, BATNA was something new. John was told that his BATNA was the key focus and driving force behind any successful negotiation. In short, his BATNA was their worst-case-but-still-acceptable resolution option.

However, the sheikhs had their own version of a BATNA, and John needed to determine how both sides could arrive at agreements that enabled each to achieve its objectives. Therein lay the rub. John was starting at a huge disadvantage because he did not grow up living in Iraqi culture, and would not be in the region forever. Even the sheikhs who sought security and stability didn't believe the U.S. was committed to long-term solutions.

John and his troops also needed to be prepared that some of the sheikhs would question the coalition forces' true motives. Some of the sheikhs thought the U.S. was in Iraq to take permanent control of the country's natural resources. As the battalion commander in charge of the city, John knew this was not the truth, but he still needed to be prepared to address this fear during negotiations.

John explained that these simulated exchanges helped him see that the negotiations were bound to be extremely tough because the two sides didn't really understand each other. John was born in New Haven, Connecticut and raised in Long Beach, California. He had lived in the United States for most of his adult life and had a very Western point of view (POV), which was hard to hide from the Iraqis. To figure out their BATNA, he had to put himself in their shoes and convince them that he had their best interests at heart and was not there to take over.

In January 2006, John—armed with his Terminator gear and two weeks' worth of scenario-based BATNA training—deployed with his 1,100 soldiers to Tal Afar. He was charged with bringing security and stability to a population of 250,000 people, who were a balanced mixture of Shia, Sunnis, and Turkemen. Given the city's diverse population, John could not look at its leaders in just one way.

This made it difficult for John to completely understand the people he was dealing with.

In January, John's first month "in country," he said he hosted meeting after meeting with the local neighborhood sheikhs at his U.S. Army command post. He was the perfect host—or so he thought—offering chai tea, sodas, and local foods.

Fast forward to February 2006. In addition to bringing safety and stability to the city, John's goal was to get the city functioning again. Toward this end, he honed in on reviving the agricultural industry and filling the water wells to full capacity. He felt those were two of the most important core services to get the city back on its feet. During his first meeting to discuss the possible reopening of agricultural plants, John recognized he needed not only to gain the trust of the city leaders, but to find the engineers, farmers, and technicians who could reopen facilities such as the local granary. This created a bit of the cart-before-the-horse situation. John needed the civilian staff to reopen facilities to help restore the safety and security in the city, but the laborers had to feel safe enough to come to work.

Naively, John underestimated the challenge of this goal. He felt his BATNA was pretty easy: I'll give you your town back, and in return, I'm asking for reduced violence and attacks against U.S. troops, Iraqi security forces, and Iraqi civilians. Going into the process, he felt he was offering the best part of the deal by bringing in security, the engineering resources of the U.S., and financial aid. He was simply asking the sheikhs to convince the populace—the fence sitters—to give the U.S. troops a chance to get the job done in relative calm and stability.

More important, John needed the sheikhs to stop playing both sides and/or providing active support to insurgents. The violent incidents John was witnessing were not decreasing. In fact, two months into his yearlong deployment, they were on the rise.

Ultimately, John realized that one of the biggest reasons he was not more successful was that he was getting only one part of the BATNA training right. He knew his own BATNA, but he did not understand the sheikhs' BATNA. What did they really want? And could he ever truly understand what they wanted, given that he was an American with a Western POV?

John believed a crucial first step to truly understanding the sheikhs' BATNA was to gain their trust. And to do this, John decided, he would become more like the Iraqis. This included what he ate, where he slept, and even what he wore. He did not become a 21st-century Lawrence of Arabia, but he did ensure that the space he operated and lived in was much more Iraqi than Californian.

The first change he made was to move the vast majority of his units inside the city of Tal Afar. This was very different from what most U.S. forces were doing in 2006; most were living in forward-operating bases behind concrete walls with barbed wires and significant barricades. These troops went into the city during the day, then returned to their safe areas to sleep in their trailers.

John couldn't understand why taking the major step of living inside the city failed to immediately win him the trust of his Iraqi counterparts. He was subjected to the dangers of the violence-prone streets alongside Iraqi security forces, and he lived among the people he was trying to protect.

Living inside Tal Afar took a high toll on John and his troops' personal comfort. They had inconsistent electricity, they did not eat hot food, and they endured the extreme weather conditions (fairly cold in the winter and extremely hot in the summer) of the high desert region. They also had no plumbing. No showers. No bathrooms. (Think camping conditions, but with the threat of mortar and sniper fire as you went to use the facilities.) They used plastic water bottles for #1. For #2, they used canisters they burned in the open-air.

John's next move was a turning point. He decided he wouldn't just live with the Iraqis, he would eat what they ate and dress as they dressed. The last step went against training that ensured he and his troops remained in their Terminator gear full-time, both for their own self-protection and to be ready to fight armed insurgents at any moment.

Here, John followed one of the tenets of *The Soul of a Deal* philosophy, which is that you can't always do things by the book. He realized that in order to gain the Iraqis' trust and get to know them better, he and his troops needed to fully live like them. This meant from that from that point forward, when he met with the sheikhs, he would go to their homes, eat whatever they offered him (including goat—all parts, eyes, everything) and drink whatever they drank. John and his troops even fasted during Ramadan.

Most important, John and his commanders took off their Terminator gear to sit cross-legged on their hosts' Persian rugs. John knew this was a risk, and that there had been numerous reports of U.S. Army-sheikh meetings being targeted by insurgents. John felt, however, that the larger goal of getting his and the sheikhs' BATNA to overlap was worth the risk. Turning the famous Vietnam phrase "we had to destroy the village in order to save it" on its head, John instituted a different approach: To save the village, he and his troops joined it.

By April, the situation had gotten significantly better. Make no mistake—when it was time to fight, John's troops fought and fought valiantly. They endured losses and casualties. However, when he negotiated with the sheikhs, John ensured that he and his leaders sat cross-legged, without their Terminator gear, and listened to the sheikhs' perspectives. This approach helped John develop "actionable intelligence" he used to target the insurgents who fired at them and planted IEDs.

By October 2006, ten months into his yearlong deployment, John was able to fully and successfully turn Tal Afar over to the Iraqi mayor, the Iraqi Army brigade commander, and the Iraqi police chief. The hospital was up and running, the water wells were pumping fresh drinking water, the schools were back in session, the markets were crowded, and the farmers had begun to farm again.

Soon, among other parts of the U.S. Army stationed in Iraq, this brand of counterinsurgency became commonplace: Join the village to save it. Take off your Terminator gear and live, eat, sleep, and sit with the Iraqis. Truly try to understand them, walk in their shoes, understand their BATNA, and win your deal.

During our conversation, John was humble. He didn't want to take credit for these Army-wide successes, but the history is clear. What he and his colleagues did in his battalion—and what the larger brigade unit did in Tal Afar and, later, Ramadi—became a model that was repeated at scale in 2007. It paved the way for the much larger success that eventually led to U.S. forces exiting Iraq in 2011.

KEY POINTS IN THIS DEAL:

- Sometimes, you have to invest weeks or months to get to know the other side—to understand their goals and objectives, and to gain their trust.

- Sometimes, you need to eat the same meals as your counterparts (metaphorically and literally).

- In certain situations, closing a deal requires taking a 180-degree turn against textbook advice and/or training.

WOULD YOU LIKE
SOME GUM WITH THAT?

In the early 90s, my first company, After Hours Software, was doing quite well with its core products, TouchBase and DateBook. During the same time, another company was also doing exceptionally well selling anti-virus and utility software under its main brand, Symantec, and its sister brand, Norton, which was started by Peter Norton, a celebrity in the early computer software industry. Known for his signature pose of standing with his arms folded, looking confident, Norton had built a very large software company that Symantec had acquired.

Symantec and Norton were primarily Windows-focused. However, they did have a few anti-virus/utility products in the Macintosh market: Symantec's Utilities for Macintosh (SUM) and Norton's Utilities for Macintosh (NUM).

As a previous Apple employee who had run a successful consulting (and now publishing) business focused on Macintosh, I was in good graces with Apple. This meant that the company sent After Hours pre-release Macintosh computers on which we could test our products.

In 1992, Apple was about to release its first legitimate laptop computer called the PowerBook. They had previously released a "portable" Macintosh, but it cost several thousand dollars, weighed about 16 pounds, and was too large to fit on the tray table of an airline seat. That effort, known as the "luggable," was not a commercial success. However, this time, their offering was priced on par with other laptops in addition to having a decent battery life and a small footprint. I had access to a pre-release PowerBook, and as I used it, I quickly realized that After Hours had an opportunity to come out with a utility package specifically designed for the computer.

Although we were already successfully shipping TouchBase and DateBook, my ambitions for the PowerBook project were quite different. After Hours was growing rapidly, and I felt that if we could get a big and swift financial win with the PowerBook product, it could be a funding source for the entire company that would help us grow our core personal productivity software business.

I clearly remember the day we came up with the list of features for our PowerBook utility product. I had taken our best engineer at After Hours, Ando, out to Castaic Lake to go jet skiing for the day. (Prior to working at After Hours, Ando worked at Now Software and developed their utility product, called Now Utilities.) Out on the lake, I got the idea for how we could make a lot of money selling our utility product to a third party and generate enough cash to fund our vision for After Hours. While Symantec had SUM and NUM, we would offer GUM: Guy's Utilities for Macintosh. I liked the idea so much I was almost giddy. The utilities would be specifically for the PowerBook, and as such, we called it GUM: PowerBook Edition.

But the idea didn't stop there. I also decided we would target Symantec to buy our product out from under us. We would use a two-pronged approach. First, we would develop a great product that could ship day and date with Apple's new PowerBook. Second, we would poke so close to home for Symantec that they would be left with almost no choice but to buy the product from us before we shipped it.

Remember that classic pose I described earlier that defined Peter Norton? We went there—straight there. The box for GUM was a picture of a guy wearing an After Hours t-shirt, blowing a bubble (yes, really), with the caption "Our GUM: Guy's Utilities for Macintosh, PowerBook Edition."

About a month before we were ready to ship GUM, I reached out to an executive I knew at Symantec. I told him we were about to ship a product, and I wanted to extend the offer to demo it for them before it hit shelves. He quickly agreed to a meeting the following week.

In preparation, I spent some time with our attorneys. We were so direct in our approach to Symantec with the name, the post, and the packaging that I wanted to make sure we weren't violating any copyrights. Fortunately for us, no one can copyright a pose or names that rhyme with Guy, so I was told we were 100% in the clear.

The meeting with Symantec was both good and bad. The good was that they really liked the product we had built and were thrilled that it was going to be able to ship the same day as the PowerBook. The bad was that they claimed our name and packaging was in violation of their copyright and trademarks. Symantec said that if we went ahead and began shipping the product, they would seek legal recourse to block us.

The next few weeks were very tense. I continued to update Symantec on our progress and informed them that we were going to proceed with shipping the product. Our first order was for 10K units. The boxes, disks, and manuals had been produced. I sent a copy of the complete package to Symantec, telling them that I was still interested in trying to work out a deal and that we wouldn't be held back by their threat of legal action.

Then, literally three days before we were scheduled to ship the first 10K units, Symantec called and said they had an offer to run past us. We met the next day, and they offered to buy the full rights for $500K. I had already decided that the product and its positioning should be worth at least $1M, and I countered with that number. I told Symantec they had 48 hours to decide, because we were about to ship.

The next day, Symantec offered to split the difference at $750K. I held firm at $1M and told them there was no way I was going to come down. Finally, the day before we were scheduled to ship, they agreed to the price tag. For $1M, they got both a great product and the security that they owned the GUM name in the marketplace.

Postscript: Symantec changed the product's name to Norton Essentials for PowerBook, and shipped it a few weeks later. And yes, a picture of Peter Norton in his signature pose was featured prominently on the cover (but not wearing an After Hours t-shirt ;-)). The proceeds of the sale to Symantec allowed After Hours to pay off some debt and put about $500K in the bank. This helped solidify the company and prepare it for its eventual sale to Adobe.

In this deal, knowing where we stood legally, having the *chutzpah* to pick the party we wanted to buy our product, and then forcing their hand ensured our success.

To a degree, this deal followed what some have referred to as "arc of new ventures." It goes like this:

1. Others ignore you.

2. Then they dismiss what you are trying to do.

3. Then they have fear, uncertainty, and doubt about you.

4. Then they recognize your value and fight you.

5. They they try and take you over.

6. Then they offer to buy you.

KEY POINT IN THIS DEAL:

- Sometimes, you can pinpoint who should acquire your business months or years in advance. In such cases, don't be shy about going after the future acquirer head-on. Poke at them in the marketplace until you get on their radar and convince them to acquire you.

CHAPTER 5
PIVOTING YOUR BUSINESS

REID HOFFMAN

YEAH, WE'RE A BANK...NO, WE'RE NOT A BANK

Reid Hoffman is one of the most amazing technology visionaries of our time. He worked at Apple early in his career and then went on to be one of the senior executives at PayPal who helped grow and sell the company to eBay. He is also the founder and still-chairman of LinkedIn; one could say he is the most "linked-in" executive in technology :-).

In addition to his operating roles, Reid has been a prolific angel investor in such massive successes as Airbnb and Twitter. He is a full partner at the Silicon Valley venture fund, Greylock Partners. Through these career highlights, Reid has amassed a fortune estimated at more than $4B. In 2014, he ranked #120 on Forbes' list of the wealthiest people in the world.

I know Reid through his philanthropic activities. He and I first met about ten years ago, and we've have had numerous engaging meetings and conversations since. Reid is one of those people with whom I have conversations that get my brain going.

For this interview, I met Reid at his office at LinkedIn's headquarters in Mountain View, California. Those who know Reid best know he is incredibly humble. He read the first few drafts of the early chapters of this book to help set the tone for our interview. As our conversation began, Reid said he wasn't sure he had any stories that were as interesting as the others he had read. Reid, I believe you are mistaken...

In technology circles, PayPal is mythological. The extremely talented executives that built the company have been satirically referred to as "the PayPal mafia."[6] In addition to Reid, founding executives include visionary Elon Musk of Tesla, SpaceX, and Solar City, and Peter Thiel, founder of the VC firm Founders Fund and the technology company Palantir. (Reid and Peter were the first outside investors in Facebook.) For this reason and because he still holds a position at LinkedIn (a public company), Reid agreed that his stories from PayPal would be the best to tell. Originally, Reid was on the board of PayPal. Eventually, he resigned to become a member of the executive management team.

Paypal was the first company to revolutionize e-commerce in the Digital Age. It was the first online service that allowed two parties to electronically exchange cash over the Internet, moving it from

---

6   https://en.wikipedia.org/wiki/PayPal_Mafia

one existing bank account directly to another. While this may seem commonplace today, in 1998 when PayPal was established, it was cutting-edge technology.

Users enjoyed Paypal's simplicity and the speed of the transactions it enabled. By simply entering their bank information, they could exchange money for goods and services from their personal computers. However, behind the scenes, PayPal was dealing with complex issues: a fierce regulatory battle and a smear campaign initiated by long-established—and threatened—banking institutions.

As Reid shared with me, when PayPal was first taking off, the company worked closely with regulators to ensure it was not classified as a "traditional bank." Such a classification would put undue strain and regulation on the company at a time when they were working to revolutionize buyer<->seller financial transactions. The early strategy (and eventual backup plan) was to get the necessary banking licenses for PayPal in the event regulators didn't see things the way its founders did.

In the end, PayPal had to rely on its backup plan. This led to the merger of PayPal with X.com, which was headed up by none other than Elon Musk. X.com held the banking licenses PayPal needed. And according to Reid, X.com had been wise to acquire them. Specifically, X.com had had the idea of buying a bank and then selling all of the customers, data, and everything else back to it except for its license. This was a clever way to acquire a banking license without the time and regulatory scrutiny that typically came with applying for one.

Shortly after acquiring X.com and its banking licenses, PayPal realized that the overhead of operating as a bank would essentially kill the company. As PayPal evolved, they grew more confident that their service, which was basically a payments service, didn't fall under the traditional banking regulations.

PayPal recognized that the primary purpose of banking regulation was consumer protection, which they were all for. However, PayPal did not handle deposits in the way traditional banks did. PayPal's service involved the real-time transfer of funds from one customer's account at an established (and regulated) bank to another's.

This meant that following its acquisition of X.com, PayPal found itself in a tricky position. It had just spent a few years convincing regulators that it was a new type of bank and that it had secured the necessary banking licenses via the X.com acquisition. Now, they were returning to the regulators, backpedaling, and saying, "We aren't a bank of any type. Therefore, no banking regulations should apply to us."

But traditional banks wanted PayPal to be regulated like they were. These banks recognized the potential market for payments processors, and went to lawmakers and pleaded with regulators to treat PayPal as a traditional bank. The banks argued that when you see a link that says, "Pay with PayPal," it is very similar to seeing "Pay with <insert bank's name here>." As such, they argued, PayPal was acting as a bank, so the same harsh regulations should apply. In fact, many traditional banks specifically sought out regulators and proactively tried to get them to shut down PayPal for illegal banking.

This presented a huge hurdle for PayPal. Not only did banks have to deal with federal government regulations, but there were state regulations as well. This meant that PayPal had to fight the issue on not just one front, but fifty. The states' biggest concern was that an entity acting as a bank could fold and lose all its customers' money. Then, the state would come under massive scrutiny. This fear is what led to various states' close inspection of PayPal.

The company's one saving grace was that even though they had a banking license, they were not operating as a bank. Specifically, they did not accept deposits or pay interest on them, and they did not loan money. Therefore, they did not need to be under the same regulations as traditional banks.

Indeed, this issue haunted PayPal up to and during their IPO. Just before the IPO was to file, PayPal received a letter from the state of Louisiana requesting that they stop their business activities, which Louisiana considered to be illegal banking. PayPal reached out to the state, only to find out that the Securities and Exchange Commissions' initial public offering regulator, who had read an article about PayPal's upcoming IPO, had asked the state to put some heat on the company. Clearly, lobbyists from traditional banking groups were working in high gear to stop PayPal's IPO.

By carefully, systematically, and thoughtfully responding to the regulators' inquiries, PayPal was able to achieve its IPO and avoid the regulations imposed on traditional banking institutions. In the end, the company's position that it was not a bank at all, which was almost undermined by its merger with X.com, was critical to its success.

Postscript: After its successful IPO in 2002, PayPal was acquired by eBay for $1.5B. In 2015, eBay announced plans to spin PayPal out into its own public company, a move that was largely pushed by investors who believed that PayPal was eBay's most valued asset.

KEY POINT IN THIS DEAL:

- Be willing to evolve your company's positioning to get the best deal/value you can, based on current economic trends and regulatory issues.

ANDREW BRACCIA

IT PAYS TO BE A SLACKER

I first met Andrew Braccia back in 2007, when he joined Accel Partners. I had just started working with Accel as a Los Angeles-based venture partner earlier that year.

Andrew was brought in because of his deep expertise, knowledge, and relationships in consumer services. He spent several years at Yahoo—his role included overseeing their search business—and Accel is known to bring in successful young businesspeople to add to the diversity of perspectives at the firm.

Andrew quickly adapted to the company culture and excelled in his transition from operator to a venture capital investor. Today, after ten years, Andrew has built an amazing portfolio—one that contains not only high-value assets but also some unicorn-level exits. Given the relatively short time he has been in the business, this is truly impressive.

Andrew's track record is stellar. Some of his key deals and exits include leading the first VC investments in such household names as Lynda.com (acquired by LinkedIn for $1.5B), MyFitnessPal (acquired by Under Armour for $475M), Slack (the core subject of this chapter), SquareSpace, and Vox Media. He also works closely with the teams at Braintree (acquired by PayPal), Etsy, UserTesting, and Cloudera.

Andrew was kind enough to sit down with me to discuss *The Soul of a Deal.* As was the case with many of my interview subjects, Andrew began by saying he wasn't sure he had a good deal story for me. But he was being too modest. After chatting for a few minutes, we both agreed that the arc that Slack had undergone during the last several years would be an exceptional story to share. The story also highlights the way Andrew likes to do deals, and it illustrates the elements of the deal-making process that are important to him.

Andrew emphasized to me that his approach to deals is different from typical VC investors'. People who have been in VC for the last few decades tend to get too caught up in the valuation of a deal—so caught up, in fact, that they risk passing on something that could be an amazing opportunity.

While Andrew is prudent and not known for overpaying in deals, he feels it's foolish to lose an opportunity over a few million-dollar difference in valuation. Unlike some VC investors, if Andrew believes deeply in a business, its team, and the vision, a few million dollars doesn't keep him from doing a deal.

Clearly, from his successes so far, Andrew's approach has proven to be tried and true. One of his biggest successes to date exemplifies his approach to deal making and helps explain why he is becoming a leader in VC deals in Silicon Valley: Slack.

Back when Andrew was an operating executive at Yahoo, he met Stewart Butterfield, the founder and CEO of Slack. It was 2005, and Yahoo was acquiring the photo-sharing site, Flickr, which Stewart had co-founded. During the next few years, the two men became colleagues and friends, developing a mutual respect for each other.

In 2009, Stewart was looking for a VC to fund his new multi-player gaming company called Tiny Speck with its planned game, Glitch. Stewart went to Andrew for funding, and Andrew agreed almost immediately to write a check for $1M to seed fund the company. It was because of his relationship with Stewart and his respect for him that Andrew was willing to make this bet so quickly.

Tiny Speck released the first version of Glitch (a massive multiplayer game) in late 2011. However, attracting users proved more difficult than they'd anticipated, and by late 2012, work on the game came to a close. But the soul of this story is not about Glitch. It's about Andrew and Stewart's collaboration and Stewart's employee management following Glitch's end.

As Andrew shared with me, it's easy for people to get along and work together when everything is going smoothly. The question he'd tackled during his time with Tiny Speck was: How does that relationship evolve and continue to work once things begin to go very wrong?

Andrew stressed that, in practice, from the very early beginning of a deal, he places his faith in the team he has backed and his relationship with that team. He truly believes in the power of collaboration, which is particularly critical during the inevitable moments of hitting bumps in the road. Trust and collaboration help all parties to be honest and objective with each other and to work together to make the right decisions. This is more effective than the alternative— namely, confrontational episodes that can cause things to go bad fast.

When the decision was made to shut down Glitch, Andrew, Stewart, and their team had an existential crisis. Tiny Speck employed nearly 50 people, its primary product was a bust, and now the management team had to figure out whether and how to the company forward. To add insult to injury, Tiny Speck was running low on funds. In most cases, a company facing these circumstances would

THE SOUL OF A DEAL

completely shut down. But what happened next at Tiny Speck was truly unique, and the outcome was remarkable.

The first thing Andrew and the company's senior team did was to go through the painful process of terminating all but about five employees, or 90% of their staff. Their next task, which shows what a mensch Stewart is, was to find jobs for all of the employees they let go. They took real action—this wasn't just lip service—and their efforts took them about two months. They launched a website called *Hire a Genius* and posted all of their laid-off employees' resumes and contact information on it. Stewart acted as a reference for all of the employees as job offers began to come in. Surely, this was painful. But Stewart handled the situation with such polish and in such a respectful manner that people took notice.

So there were Andrew and Stewart with a company that was running out of cash and had only five of its original 50 employees. But the two were unwilling to throw in the towel. They pulled themselves up by their bootstraps and started exploring ways to restart the company—essentially from scratch.

Stewart and his team at Tiny Speck developed Slack without the intention of making it a product. They simply built a toolset to help them efficiently communicate and collaborate. Basically, they customized IRC (a tool that had been around for a few decades) and built workflow management on top of that.

Stewart believes that much of Slack's success is due to the fact that they did not realize they were building a winning product. It's a point he emphasizes. Slack began as a secondary thing. It was a toolset for their existing team. They didn't dwell on every feature or overthink the details—they simply built what worked for them. At the time, they had no idea what Slack would become.

Little did Stewart or his management team know how helpful Slack would be during the painful exercise of letting 90% of their staff go. Nor did they know Slack would give them the courage to start again. After the dissolution of Tiny Speck, Stewart and his remaining team realized the internal tool could be helpful to any other company trying to manage complex, real-time communications. It was more effective than traditional email and text messages.

With Slack as Tiny Speck's flagship product, Andrew and Stewart began to rebuild the company. And they achieved far more success than they'd ever imagined they would with Glitch. Stewart and his team began hiring again, and Tiny Speck quickly exceeded 50 employees. As of the time of this interview, the company employed approximately 500 people (with several early Tiny Speck employees making up that group).

Slack has become so ingrained in startup and technology culture that it has achieved Silicon Valley-lexicon status. "I'll slack you that information," has become a common phrase, as has "Check your slack for an update." In effect, Tiny Speck created an entirely new communications platform that, four years after its launch, has become one of the fastest-growing services out there.

Slack is now considered one of Silicon Valley's biggest current successes. As of this writing, Slack has raised more than $500M and has a valuation approaching $3B. It all started with that $1M investment Andrew was willing to commit to Stewart back in 2009, when he had no idea just how transformative the company and what it created would be for an entire industry.

KEY POINTS IN THIS DEAL:

- If you bet on an extremely talented team, you may end up with a big win even if the original vision, plan, or product is not successful.

- You have to know when to pivot. And in pivoting, you may have to make very hard decisions such as going from 50 employees down to 5 and then rebuilding the company from scratch.

CHAPTER 6
CLEVER ASSERTIVENESS

SOMETIMES, YOU HAVE TO SEND CUPCAKES

I served as the chief strategy officer of RealNetworks from 2002-2006. During that time, the company took on what would be one of my favorite projects: the Rhapsody music service. In 2003, I led the $36M acquisition of the company that founded Rhapsody, Listen.com, and brought the service into the family of RealNetworks' products.

My intuition about subscription music services being the wave of future was right, but I was about a decade too early. In most cases, being too early is the same as being wrong. In fact, in 2016, a whopping 13 years after RealNetworks acquired Rhapsody, the revenue generated by subscription music services finally outpaced all other forms of music distribution. Today, the landscape is filled with digital music subscription services including Spotify, Beats (now owned by Apple), SoundCloud, Rhapsody, Tidal, and others.

I was so convinced that subscription music services were the future because of the wide variety they afford music-loving consumers and the amazing value that really has. For $10/month, you have access to the world's music in an unlimited and unrestricted way. You can play it on your laptop, your smartphone, your tablet, or your wireless home stereo. It is this last platform—the wireless home stereo—where subscription services' value proposition really shines.

In 2002, a small startup called Sonos was formed in Santa Barbara. Sonos was a pioneer in the home wireless audio space; theirs was a breakthrough product that came with a hefty price tag. The product itself was a combination of amplifiers and wireless receivers that could power your speakers and sync the playback of your favorite songs across multiple rooms. Sonos also sold a controller that looked like an iPod on steroids (recall the Apple products of 2004). It included a small LCD screen and a scroll wheel to search for all of your music.

The founder and CEO of Sonos, John Macfarlane (a serial entrepreneur), had a great vision, a talented engineering and hardware team, and strong financial backing—all the makings of a successful company. The first version of Sonos, however, was useful only if you had a library of thousands of songs. While high-end audiophiles had such libraries, average music consumers did not. They simply didn't digitize their collections of hundreds of CD's or spend thousands of dollars purchasing music from the iTunes store.

Early on, I recognized the connection between Rhapsody and Sonos. They were a match made in musical heaven. Rhapsody shined because customers could play any music they wanted on-demand, anywhere in their house. Sonos shined because customers had access to tens of thousands of tracks. Seeing the potential in their combination, I set out to form a partnership between the two companies.

At the Consumer Electronics Show in 2004, my team and I met with John McFarlane and his senior team in the RealNetworks suite. We showed Rhapsody off like proud parents, and they did the same with Sonos. It was very clear to both of us that this was a perfect fit, and we began in earnest to set up a partnership.

Within a few months, we struck a mutually beneficial deal whereby Sonos would feature Rhapsody as their exclusive music service, and Rhapsody would promote Sonos as the "whole home audio solution." No money would directly change hands. Instead, we would get a happy paying subscriber, and Sonos would get a customer who would buy several zones' worth of equipment so they could play Rhapsody throughout their house.

This partnership turned out to be one of the more meaningful deals for each of the relatively young companies, as it allowed us to stand out. The Rhapsody/Sonos customers were the best and most loyal customers we had. In subscription services, a HUGE issue is determining the customer's lifetime. Most subscription services average about a year, and then people churn out (cancel). This was typically the case with Rhapsody users. However, the Rhapsody/Sonos users had a lifetime average of 4+ years, a whopping 400% increase over standard subscribers. Even as early as 2005 and 2006, these metrics confirmed our suspicions that streaming music services were the future.

Fast forward slightly more than a decade, and this is no longer a theory. Reality took much longer to set in than it should have. Over and over, I've learned that technological revolution happens much faster than consumer adoption.

During the years between roughly 2007 and 2012, when the streaming model really took off, Rhapsody was surpassed by services such as Spotify and SoundCloud. Our initial exclusive deal with Sonos lasted only a year. Now, Sonos brokers the sale of most of these music services, reserving their best placement for the highest bidder.

The fact that Rhapsody didn't remain #1 still pains me. Although this is not the point of this chapter, I ask you, dear reader, to humor me for a moment so I can share my view of why it happened.

During the last ten years, Rhapsody has been either fully owned by RealNetworks (as it was during my tenure) or partially owned as a part of a joint venture (as it is today). During this time, Rhapsody's owners have needed to disclose their revenue, profit, and loss, and this reporting has had a strong impact on the company's stock price.

In 2006, Spotify came onto the scene and focused exclusively on growing its subscriber base at any cost. As of this writing, Spotify has raised a whopping $1.5B in funding, and Rhapsody has changed its name to Napster, an asset it bought years ago.

Sonos, meanwhile, has emerged as one of the most transformative consumer electronics companies on the Internet. They have raised close to half a billion dollars in funding. They are widely accepted as the leader in wireless streaming audio, having beaten longtime players such as Bose to the punch. They now market themselves in the occasional television ad and print.

With the widespread adoption of smartphones and the growth of the app marketplace, Sonos discontinued their own iPod-like controller several years ago. Instead, they developed free controller apps for both iPhone and Android devices. (They could afford to do this because an average whole-home Sonos system cost upward of a few thousand dollars.) This was a very strategic and risky move. They knew they would get decimated in the controller market, so they chose to decimate themselves.

At the same time, Sonos continued to evolve from an "Internet-controlled amplifier" to Internet-controlled speakers that range in price from $199-$399 per speaker. Much of Sonos' success has to be attributed to their founder and CEO, John Macfarlane, the gentleman with whom I shared several meals ten years ago when we were both new to the game.

When I formed HelloTech at the end of 2014, part of my vision was to sell the best of breed home products, and Sonos was at the top of my list of products to sell. I thought, "This should be pretty straightforward. I know John from back in the day, when we broke bread and cut our teeth together. I'll just reach out to him and ask that HelloTech become a distributor for Sonos." I thought we'd be off to the races. But I couldn't have been more wrong.

With the kind of success Sonos had achieved comes great responsibility and burden. Everyone wants something from you. CEOs in John's position routinely get hundreds of emails a day, compromising their ability to triage and focus on the things that would make the biggest difference to their companies. During the time I was attempting to connect with John in 2014, I believe he was overwhelmed, and that this was why I could not get him to respond to my emails for two to three months.

Even though I empathized with John's position, don't get me wrong—it was very frustrating. I even solicited the assistance of a close friend who was still involved with Sonos (and one of the top ten most influential people in the music industry), Marc Geiger, the Head of Worldwide Music for William Morris Endeavor. I told him what I was hoping for in terms of distribution and asked if he could ping John on my behalf. Marc was a great resource. Just a few days later, he sent me an email along with an email John had sent him apologizing for not getting back to me and saying I should send him another note, and he would reply.

Following Marc's suggestion, I sent John another note, cc'ing Marc. I outlined what HelloTech was all about and how we wanted to feature the Sonos product line. I told John we weren't looking for anything special, just the standard distribution deal terms. Certainly this time I would hear back, I thought. Crickets. My emails continued to go unanswered.

Then, in early 2015, this situation escalated from an annoyance to an actual problem. We were closing additional funding for HelloTech, and I had banked on having a good connection with Sonos and making them one of our first partners. Investors started asking me if the deal with Sonos was done. Of course, I had to tell the truth. I said the deal was not done, but I was confident that it would be soon. (Truthfully, at that point, I had some doubts. And frankly, I was very disappointed in John.)

Sure, it had been years since John and I had corresponded, but it wasn't as if we were distant acquaintances. We had met several times: in Santa Barbara for breakfast, in Seattle, in Vegas, etc. I needed to close this deal. I also needed to detach myself from my personal feelings, which almost never help get a deal done. I needed to get creative and appeal to John's guilt. And then I had the cupcake idea.

I found a local high-end cupcake bakery in Santa Barbara. I arranged to have 50 of their best cupcakes delivered to Sonos the following Monday morning with a note that said, "Hey John, remember me from the Rhapsody days? I have been trying to get a deal with Sonos for months with no response. Hopefully, this will sweeten your memory to the deal that was so important to us a decade ago, when we were both getting started in this game. Please share these with your senior staff and other team members."

The following Monday, in the early afternoon, I received a call from John's assistant. She wanted to let me know that John was out of town for the day but appreciated my thoughtfulness and that the cupcakes had been shared around the office. She also promised Sonos would be in touch with me soon, and within 48 hours, I received an email from Sonos' head of worldwide sales. He said he would connect me with their head of California dealers, who would be happy to set up HelloTech as a dealer.

The most important lesson in this story is to not take things personally when someone doesn't get back to you. Sure, it's frustrating. And I was frustrated. But in the end, John wasn't trying to ignore me; he was simply buried under running the beast he had built. I needed to see past my hurt feelings, get creative, and get in his face (in a positive way) to make this deal happen. Sometimes, you have to send cupcakes ;-).

KEY POINTS IN THIS DEAL:

- Technological advancement happens faster than consumer adoption, so pace yourself and your expectations when doing a deal that involves cutting-edge technology.

- Private companies are not under the same scrutiny as public companies, so they can be more aggressive (i.e., increase spending even after losing tens of millions of dollars) in their pursuit of market share.

- Just because you did meaningful business with someone in the past doesn't mean they will give you due respect on a totally different deal in the future.

- Sometimes, to get a deal unstuck, you have to be creative and personal and send gifts or gags to the other party.

FACING THE MUSIC...
IN FRONT OF CONGRESS

It was 1999, and the file-sharing service Napster was growing like gangbusters. Napster was a great service for consumers. Not only could you access all of your favorite music for free, but bootlegs and live recordings that had never been released for purchase were also available.

Napster used what was called a peer-to-peer file sharing network, whereby every person who used Napster became a broadcaster. If you downloaded a Beatles' song, the next person who wanted it could get it from your computer if Napster deemed they had a solid connection to you. The peer-to-peer file sharing structure was the legal screen that Napster tried to hide behind. Clearly, something was not right about being able to download all of the music you wanted— some of which had never even been officially released—for free.

In 1999, the RIAA, the industry group that represented all music labels, launched an effort to get the courts to deem Napster illegal and shut it down. The same year, I was contracted by RealNetworks to do digital media work. I had gotten to know the company's Founder and Chairman/CEO Rob Glaser during my tenure at Disney, and he invited me to help RealNetworks by becoming the acting CEO of MusicNet. This, if you recall, was the first of its kind legitimate music streaming service, partnering with three of the top five music labels.

RealNetworks had been working on developing MusicNet to varying degrees for a few years. The success of the enterprise hinged on licensing deals with major record labels that would enable the company to sell digital music over the Internet. During the late

1990s, inertia was causing music labels to move very slowly on this front.

I had two main responsibilities at MusicNet: build a technology platform and website that allowed for the access and distribution of digital music (including the use of something called a DRM, or Digital Rights Manager, so that files couldn't be shared) and get the major labels to license their catalogs of music to the company.

Frankly, the technology was by far the easier task. It was within our control, and our systems advanced rapidly alongside the Internet's growth. RealNetworks already had audio codecs and DRM technology we could leverage to build out the MusicNet platform.

Licensing the music, on the other hand, was totally out of our control. Sure, we had meeting after meeting with all of the usual suspects—at the time, these were Universal, Sony, Warner, EMI, and Bertelsmann—but we couldn't force them to license their catalogs to us. Our pitch was pretty straightforward: "Guys, you are getting slammed by Napster. We are the good guys. We can put a system in place to provide music in a protected space where users have to pay to get access to any of the files. We can track exactly which artists' music is downloaded and played, and then pay the labels their pro rata shares based on which songs/artists are being played the most."

Most of the conversations also involved exploratory discussions around entering into a joint venture with some or all of the music labels. The idea was that we would not only offer a service to counteract Napster, but also bring revenue to the music labels and build a company with equity value in which they could participate. It should have been a no-brainer for them. But as with most things having to do with the music labels, there were no "no-brainers," and it seemed we were getting nowhere.

Then, all of a sudden, it was as if the dam broke. During a single week, all of the labels were breathing down our neck, saying they wanted to finalize a licensing agreement as soon as possible. They offered to fly their business development groups to Seattle to meet at our headquarters or host us at their respective locations. They told us they wanted to do a deal, and they wanted to move fast.

There was a lot of jockeying that week because all of the labels also bit on our JV idea, saying they were "ready to go." First, we thought we'd partner with Universal. Then Sony seemed to move to the front of the line. Then Warner Music. Back and forth it went, at which point we found ourselves in active and progressive conversations with Warner, EMI, and Bertelsmann. Much to our surprise, they all told us they wanted to get deals signed within a week and that we should send our entire team to New York prepared to work night and day until we until we had signed licensing and JV agreements in hand. It seemed too good to be true, but we were rolling with the punches.

Over the next few days, we were able to figure out what was going on and why our typically inertia-laden friends wanted to move so rapidly. Napster was exploding, all of the labels were suing, and the CEO of AOL/Time Warner Dick Parsons and other media company leaders were scheduled to testify before Congress about Napster's illegitimacy. They were seeking an immediate injunction to shut Napster down. Word on the street was that Congress didn't feel that the music industry was doing enough to offer a legitimate competitor to Napster. And there it was—the spark and momentum. Dick Parsons didn't want to testify before Congress with nothing but his dick in his hand. He desperately wanted to show how the music labels were working diligently to offer a Napster alternative. Now that we understood what the trigger was, we were better able to work toward closing a deal. The next several days were a blur.

We took up office space in a New York City high-rise that housed highbrow law firm that represented AOL/Time Warner. Negotiations were very tricky due to antitrust concerns. Warner Music, EMI, and Bertelsmann all working together to get MusicNet formed could be perceived as monopolistic and anti-competitive.

As such, RealNetworks needed to have separate 1:1 negotiations with each of the three labels. Four war rooms were set up for this purpose: one for Real, and one for each of the three labels. The rules were stringent. Real could not be in more than one label meeting at a time. People from the three labels were not allowed to go into each other's war room. Also, AOL, which was signing up to distribute the MusicNet product, received its own war room and was banned from entering the others'.

Those 72 hours were a ridiculous flurry of deal making and partner orchestration. It was unlike anything I had ever seen or have seen since. We essentially camped out on that law firm's floor for three days, breaking late at night to get some sleep. Food was brought in so that we didn't have to leave the office. We (Real) went from one war room to another, not able to tell the label we were meeting with where we had made progress with their competitors or where we were still stuck.

Things were so crazy. I remember the general counsel for Real had just given birth. She needed to get a break every few hours to go to the restroom and pump breast milk. The night before the Congressional hearing, Dick Parsons himself came into the room to help us deal with some fragments of the AOL deal that were threatening to hold up some of the maze of other deals being struck.

As we neared the end of the three days, the law firm set up a new war room that housed copies of all of the agreements to be signed by all of the parties to give birth to MusicNet. There were the three separate and individual licensing deals between MusicNet and its label partners. There was the distribution agreement that allowed Real to distribute the MusicNet product. There was the distribution agreement with AOL that allowed them to distribute the MusicNet product. All in all, I remember there were about 15 agreements that needed to be signed. Late at night, before the hearing in Washington, we consummated all of the agreements necessary to officially create MusicNet and establish its initial budget, its initial funding, and its initial distribution.

Postscript: Dick Parsons testified before Congress the next day, citing the newly formed MusicNet as a show of good faith that the major music labels were providing a legal alternative to Napster. Shortly thereafter, the injunction against Napster was issued, and the music-sharing service was forced to shut down. The two main drivers that got this deal done were a hardcore deadline and pressure from government authorities.

Post-postscript: In the end, the labels did the deals because they felt forced to. But inertia still held on and hurt the newly formed MusicNet. While the labels agreed to provide content to MusicNet, they provided very little from top-tier talent when the service first launched. Thus, the $9.99 service was met with a thud when it was launched by Real and AOL. The lesson here is that if your counterpart on a deal is essentially forced into it, they are going to provide only the bare minimum necessary to make good on it. In many cases, these deals are not worth doing.

KEY POINT IN THIS DEAL:

- To the greatest extent possible, understand the other party's motivation for getting your deal done, especially if there is a time-related incentive on the other party's side. If you can discern this information, you'll have a big leg up in negotiating the best possible deal.

VIGNETTE: GETTING THE DOC
TO REMOVE THE IV

So there I was in the hospital, recovering from the removal of most of my colon (yes, I have only half a colon, I'm sorry to say :-)). I was surviving on nothing but a clear liquid diet and an IV drip for a few days as my intestines healed and grew back together.

Surviving on nothing but clear liquids was incredibly hard. Then, early in the morning of the third day, the surgeon told me he was going to approve the removal of my IV, which meant I could eat some food and nourish myself. I was thrilled. Finally, I was going to be able to eat something. As the day went on, I kept asking the nurses whether they saw the orders to remove my IV and whether they could take it out. There ain't a lot to do sitting in the hospital, so I was pretty persistent in pestering the nurses.

By mid-afternoon, the head nurse explained to me that the doctor hadn't noted removal of the IV on my chart, and until he came back (which wasn't expected until the next morning) and approved it, there was nothing she could do. I was pissed. And hungry. I decided that I was going to take matters into my own hands.

I was in the UCLA Hospital, which is next door to the UCLA Medical Center, where my surgeon's office was located. I wasn't going to sit by idly and wait an entire day, so I moved my IV onto a pole with wheels, put on a hospital gown that hung open around my bare naked ass, and I took off for the surgeon's office.

Walking through a hospital with an IV on a pole with your ass showing is not that unusual. But when daylight broke as I walked across the courtyard, I started getting stares. I made my way into the medical center and nonchalantly got in the elevator (yes, bare ass still showing) with everyone else in their street clothes.

I can still remember the look on the receptionist's face when I walked into the surgeon's waiting room with my notepad in hand. "What are you doing in here!" she exclaimed. "You're making our other patients uncomfortable!" I calmly explained the situation and told her I would leave as soon as the surgeon noted the order to remove my IV.

It took no more than five minutes before the surgeon called me into his office and reprimanded me for leaving the hospital like that (I couldn't give a shit). But he signed the paperwork. Then it was back to the elevator for me, across the courtyard, and up to my room, where the nurses summarily removed the IV and asked me what I wanted to eat. Within the hour, I was feasting on a bowl of Cream of Wheat.

Postscript: Sometimes, to close a deal, you have to be willing to expose your ass.

DAVIS GUGGENHEIM

GIVE SOMETHING UP TO GET
MORE IN RETURN

Davis Guggenheim is one of the most sought after documentary filmmakers working today. The 54-year-old won an academy award for *An Inconvenient Truth* in 2007 and has created such inspiring films as *Teach, Waiting for Superman,* and most recently, *He Named Me Malala.*

Davis was kind enough to take time out of the early development phase of *He Named Me Malala* to talk about his deal-making process. Like so many people I've interviewed, Davis began our conversation by saying he didn't really think he had any stories for *The Soul of a Deal* because he saw himself as an artist and a filmmaker, not a businessperson. However, once our conversation began, as had happened in my other interviews, Davis quickly recalled a deal he'd made when shooting one of his documentaries that he believes was one of the keys to his success.

In Hollywood, once you are successful and powerful enough, you can ask for "final cut privilege," which means that you can do pretty much whatever you want with a movie and have final say in what remains in the movie and what goes. In most cases, the director of the film has final cut. But sometimes, when there is a super A-list actor involved in a movie, they can also be given this privilege.

The artistry Davis brings to creating documentary films is different from traditional fiction filmmakers'. He finds a compelling true story that people will find interesting and then tells that story in a captivating way. Many films ago, Davis recognized that getting meaningful access to the human subject of a film, including the intimate or difficult details of the subject's personal life, is the best way to make a documentary not only compelling but also deeply personal.

As Davis' star was rising to "final cut" level with the studios that financed his films, he had the simple but highly creative and altogether brilliant idea to offer the subjects of his documentaries an equal part in final cut right up front, before they even asked. Part of the reason this was so powerful was that most of the people in Hollywood are maniacally focused on getting more and more power as they advance in the industry. In Davis' case, once he achieved this level of power, he did the opposite and effectively gave up unilateral control of his films by inviting the subjects of his documentaries to share that power with him.

By offering the subjects of his films the power to share in final cut decisions, Davis found—time and time again—that they let him into much more of their stories. And this increased his films' power. Davis' subjects would drop their guard during shooting, knowing they would later have a chance to come in and request that anything they wanted to be removed be removed.

As Davis explained to me, making a movie of any kind, especially a documentary, is a leap of faith. Giving someone a voice allows for both the addition and the removal of personal details. The brilliance of Davis' idea has manifested in the results. First, the subjects open up much more than they originally thought they would. Second, as the creation of the documentary progresses, Davis has noted, his subjects rarely end up asking him to cut any detail that really matters to the story.

Sharing final cut, which most of Hollywood would regard as a loss of power, yields Davis more intimate and compelling stories, the telling of which is the ultimate goal of documentary filmmaking.

KEY POINT IN THIS DEAL:

- Though you may be in an industry such as Hollywood, where most people believe "the more you get, the more you get," you may be able to get more overall by giving something up, especially if you think outside the box.

CHAPTER 7
NOT NOW

THERESIA GOUW

"NO" REALLY MEANT "NOT YET."
HOW TO GET TO $3.5B.

I first met Theresia when I was an executive at RealNetworks, and her then-firm, Accel Partners, was our lead investor. She and I instantly hit it off and became fast friends. Since that time (more than ten years now), we have worked on many investments together. She is a successful venture capital investor and one of the few female partners in an industry that is 95% male.

Theresia started her career as an engineer as I did, and this gave her a tremendous foundation for investing in technology companies. Named to the *Forbes* Midas List several times, Theresia was a partner at Accel for 15 years and led many successful exits including Trulia, Imperva, Kosmix, PeopleSupport, and LearnVest. Unlike many VCs, Theresia has been willing to make early bets on companies during their seed round. She also led the first rounds for several thriving private companies, including HotelTonight, BirchBox, and ForeScout.

Theresia presently serves as a treasurer of Brown University. She is also the vice-chair of DonorsChoose.org and she co-teaches a course on venture capital at Stanford's Graduate School of Business. We sat down one morning in Palo Alto to discuss the "soul" of some of her deals. In particular, we touched on one of her biggest successes, Trulia, which was acquired by competitor Zillow in July of 2014 for $3.5B.

Theresia first met Pete and Sami, the co-founders of Trulia, back when they were both students at Stanford. Around that time, the partnership at Accel had decided they wouldn't invest in a company unless the founders were full-time. Since Pete and Sami were still students, an investment in what was then called RealWide was put on hold. (Theresia didn't love the name.)

Theresia had been looking into the real estate sector, specifically into vertical search, and had spent time exploring startups: some in residential, some in commercial, and some in vacation. This strategy was part of a broader approach taken at Accel Partners they'd termed "Prepared Minds." Every year, the team came up with a thesis about which categories they believed were ripe for investment and growth. The "Prepared Minds" strategy allowed them to focus on certain areas and build strategic knowledge while also determining which categories were not of interest. This helped them better manage their time and effort.

Theresia was specifically interested in Pete and Sami's idea because their approach was to use a massive amount of data (which had recently become available on the Internet) to provide comprehensive information and prices on residential real estate listings to consumers in a very user-friendly way. There were established safe havens; copyright precedents were in place that allowed for this general approach and use of Internet data.

Right around the same time, Zillow, a RealWide competitor, began to get some good buzz and traction. Zillow pioneered a feature they called Zestimates that provided informed estimates of the price of any piece of residential real estate in the United States. This feature landed them a cover piece in *Fortune* magazine and millions of users who wanted to see the Zestimate of their home and voyeuristically view the value of others'.

Theresia stayed in touch with Pete and Sami until they graduated from business school in June 2005. At that point, she was able to go ahead and try to make an investment work. By September 2005, Trulia (RealWide's new name), raised a Series A investment of $4.5M at a $11M pre-money valuation. This worked for both parties in that Accel ended up with about 30% of the company, and the founders got their double-digit million-dollar valuation.

The company grew quite well from an audience and user perspective. It was able to raise its Series B from Sequoia with participation from Accel, and in early 2008, they raised their Series C from existing investors. The capital markets bust happened during the late summer of 2008, and the real estate market and its associated industries subsequently endured some serious rough patches. This was a critical juncture for Trulia, which was able to manage through the real estate crisis and find new successes by tapping into the distressed sale and foreclosure market.

In 2010, Zillow had a very successful IPO. Although Trulia was doing well, they were still 12-24 months away from going public. Given that both companies were in the same space, combining the two made logical sense. When Zillow approached Trulia about a possible merger in 2011, the board of directors at Trulia decided to move forward and enter into in discussions. After extensive conversations between the companies' executives and their boards of directors, the two concluded they couldn't come to terms on a deal that would work for both of them. As such, Trulia declined the acquisition offer from Zillow.

An important note, however, was that both companies negotiated in a very respectful and professional manner. The key lesson here is to always take the high road, even when the deal doesn't go through. There is rarely, if ever, value in being difficult or disrespectful when a deal doesn't work out. In many cases, it's just a matter of timing that determines its success.

This indeed proved to be the case with Zillow and Trulia. During the next few years, both companies continued to grow their audiences and their revenues. Both Zillow and Trulia were able to fend off legacy companies in the space such as Realtor.com in addition to various upstarts that tried to capture some of the consumer real estate market share. In 2012, Trulia had a successful IPO. Now, both companies public and had strong share prices. This proved to the market and their competitors that each was a viable, long-term business.

In 2014, Zillow made another foray into the merger discussions with Trulia. Once again, the executive management teams were interested enough to engage their respective boards of directors. Theresia was an active advisor on the merger for the Trulia team. While the factors in this round were similar to those in the first, including the strategic reasons why a combined Zillow/Trulia made sense, the dollar values were now almost 10X greater than they had been in 2010 because both companies had grown so substantially.

Trulia's decision to remain on good terms with Zillow paid off when the companies came back to the negotiating table. As Theresia explained to me, even if a deal is falling apart, you want to remain on good terms with the other side. "Even if you never ever want to combine with that other company, or take money from that other company, they are clearly someone in your same business category, in your industry, so you don't want to make an enemy unnecessarily."

When Zillow made the offer, Pete was still the CEO of Trulia and spoke to each of his board members individually to "take their temperature" on the offer. (This is often how a CEO will socialize a very strategic decision. By the time of the board meeting, all of the negotiating is done, and the board vote is a *fait accompli*.) In Pete's conversation with Theresia, she turned the question back on him and said, "Pete, you know what you think is a fair value for the company today in a way that is not discounting the future upside too much and also in a way that is factoring in future risk. If you think now is the right time to make the move, I will support you."

Given the previous negotiations between the two companies, the mutual respect they had for each other, and the ongoing relationships that existed between various board members, the deal came together very quickly—in about one month. Once completed, Trulia received $3.5B in stock, and Zillow became the dominant player in consumer real estate. Comparatively, Accel initially invested $4.5M for almost 30% of the company at a $11M pre-money valuation. With this deal, Accel's $4.5M investment was worth more than $1B—roughly 300X more.

KEY POINTS IN THIS DEAL:

- Often, mergers take the form of informal discussions over multiple occasions before they actually materialize. Don't view M&A discussions as a waste if a deal doesn't come to fruition; they could lay the groundwork for a future deal.

- It is critical to stay on good terms when a deal doesn't come together because, in many cases, there will be another bite at the apple in the future.

JODIE MCLEAN

LET SOMEONE ELSE BE THE BAD COP

I was fortunate enough to be introduced to Jodie McLean via a mutual friend, Sheryl Sandberg, the COO of Facebook. I had asked Sheryl about being interviewed for this book, but there is a strict no-interview policy regarding any deals at Facebook. Sheryl graciously introduced me to Jodie McLean, who was president and chief investment officer of EDENS when we first met and is now the company's CEO.

EDENS is a $6B commercial real estate developer privately held by three main blue-chip investors. Jodie first joined the company in 1990. Since then, she has risen in the ranks and negotiated over $12B worth of transactions.

As Jodie and I discussed which of her stories might be most helpful to readers of this book, she explained that, in her opinion, the most important aspect you must bring to any negotiation is empathy for the other side. She said, "If you can empathize with the other side by understanding what is important to them and why, then you can help structure a deal that meets the other party's objectives while achieving their goals as well as your own."

Every deal has a lifecycle to it, and every deal has a beginning, a middle, and an end. (Hopefully, it culminates in a signed agreement). Jodie said she begins each deal's process by listening and trying to understand the other party's objective for entering into the deal and why. As important as developing empathy in this way, Jodie also never takes her eye off what she wants and needs in the deal before she walks into the first meeting.

One tactic Jodie uses to understand and empathize with the other side is to ask, at the very beginning of the deal, "What is the ideal outcome for the other party if this transaction is successful?" By listening to and appreciating the answer to that question, more often than not, Jodie and her team are able to consummate a deal and end up with a win-win for both parties.

Jodie further explained that it is not unusual for her to do repeat business or have long-term relationships with people she does deals with. Several negotiations have been the beginning of a decade or multi-decade partnership, wherein both parties have a stake in a future real estate development project. Given the long-term nature of her typical deals, the need for true win-wins is critically important.

In addition to empathy, one of Jodie's key tenets of deal making is that you MUST be willing to walk away from any deal if you don't get what you need out of it. Many people get caught up in the process and become so focused on completing the deal that they may not get what they truly need. They give in on a few minor things at the start and eventually let go of original terms of paramount importance. As such, they end up with a deal they should never have moved ahead with.

The particular story Jodie decided to share with me concerned a very successful deal and partnership with a major international company. The deal was intriguing because it actually needed to die a few times (much like the RealNetworks/Microsoft settlement) before it got to the point where both sides were able to achieve their goals.

Jodie learned to gauge when there was an opportunity for progress versus when it made sense to let the deal go away for a time.

This deal was located in a major East Coast MSA, in a county with a highly educated and a densely populated city. Jodie had her eye on a massive mixed-use development there, but in order to achieve her vision, she needed to acquire the existing property from the corporation that owned it. (I'll refer to this corporation simply as "Company.") This asset was part of Company's national chain, and those in charge of the chain had a reputation for being particularly tough negotiators.

The asset Jodie needed to make her development a success was like "a hole in the donut" of some of EDENS' other holdings; without acquiring that center, they could not do the entire project. Adding the property to their portfolio would allow them to develop a very compelling, high-end multi-million-square-foot development. But the question Jodie faced was this: How do you get someone to agree to sell you their property at the right price when they're not motivated and don't seem to need the cash?

All of this took place during the economic boom that preceded the real estate crisis of 2008.

Jodie and her team put together what they thought was an aggressive offer for the Company's property. In response, the Company said they were going to shop the deal and asked Jodie to engage in a negotiation to improve upon the offer EDENS had made.

This is where Jodie's discipline and experience really paid off. She knew her offer was more than fair, and that nobody would actually close with a more compelling one. Armed with that knowledge, she decided to politely decline to engage in the negotiations, wished the seller the best of luck with their sale, and walked away from the deal. It was a brilliant strategy. She knew that the offers the seller received would be superior to hers, but that they buyers would not be able to close.

Effectively, she let other buyers inform Company of the value of her deal by allowing them to go ahead and walk, all the while sitting on the sidelines knowing that at some point, they would be back. Jodie and EDENS were not the party to tell Company they weren't being reasonable. Instead, EDENS let other interested parties be the bad cops.

Eventually, Company did contract with another buyer. But Jodie knew the deal wouldn't go through, and that the buyer would educate Company on the true value of their real estate. Jodie's style is based on her principle of always being up front and direct with the other side by saying, "This is the best I can do. If it's not enough for you, I fully understand, and there is no harm in walking away from my deal."

Fast forward to a year later, when Company called Jodie back. As she predicted, their deal with the other buyer had fallen through. Jodie knew this dynamic had created strong leverage for her side of the negotiations. It had been clear to both parties that Company wouldn't return to the table with EDENS unless they had exhausted all other options.

Jodie put together a comprehensive plan that would allow EDENS to put the project's full acreage under contract and organize for new and proper entitlements. The plan allowed for EDENS to achieve its objectives while also allowing Company to retain their building as part of the mixed-use development project, which met

Company's primary long-term objective. Jodie had created a win-win situation for both sides

When all was said and done, EDENS had to invest close to $75 million in the site prior to construction, expending the funds on adjacent land purchases, design, zoning, and entitlements. EDENS assembled the parcels adjacent to the one Company would retain, completed the re-zoning, and, in order to satisfy Company, positioned the asset on the site with the highest visibility.

Although they were under contract with Company, EDENS had not yet closed on the site acquisition when *BAM!* the 2008 financial crisis hit. Suddenly, it no longer made sense to purchase the land and move forward as previously planned. However, as a private company with just a few institutional investors, EDENS had more flexibility to move forward during this tumultuous time than some of their public counterparts did. Even in the midst of the crisis, Jodie strongly believed that what she had was a truly special parcel of real estate, and she wanted to move forward with the purchase.

Then, something happened that made the deal much more important for Company and, as such, put Jodie in a much stronger negotiating position. She told me she vividly remembers the day. She opened the newspaper and read that Company had significant payments to make. Overnight, she went from dealing with an organization that needed little or no cash to one that needed it immediately. Being empathic allowed her to adjust her negotiating position with Company to address their new most important need, which was cash—not the asset.

Despite the fact that the country was in turmoil, Jodie knew the crisis would not last forever and that she had an opportunity to develop a truly exciting piece of real estate. She called Company and set up a meeting for the next week. She wasn't taking advantage of the other side (something she believes is key in a win-win negotiation), but rather seizing upon a narrow window of opportunity to purchase the property from a seller that had been cash-rich but was now focused on the potential proceeds from a sale to EDENS.

Jodie went to the meeting and sat with Company's advisors and general counsel. She presented the binders and documents and stated that EDENS was prepared to start construction. This put Company on notice to proceed with their part of the project. Company's advisors quickly cut down the conversation. They bluntly stated they had no intention of proceeding with their part of the project, which put them in breach of the companies' agreement.

Seizing upon the unique opportunity the real estate crisis had created, Jodie was able to negotiate—and significantly reduce—the transaction's final cost. It was a two-week moment in time when cash was king, and Company was in need of it. Jodie's ability to recognize what was most important to Company at that particular moment in time presented a great opportunity for her.

Ultimately, Jodie's project was a tremendous success. By having empathy for the other side, knowing when to walk away, knowing when to let other people deliver bad news (the true worth of the property), and knowing when to come back to the table prepared to be aggressive and get something done, Jodie masterfully negotiated a deal that satisfied all parties and culminated in a massive success for EDENS.

KEY POINT IN THIS DEAL:

- If you are in a complex negotiation with another
  party who is very sophisticated but also has an
  unrealistic view of the value of their side of the
  deal, encourage them to work with others who can
  set them straight. Let those others illuminate for
  the party you're dealing with how unrealistic their
  demands are, and then reenter negotiations once
  they've internalized the truth.

THE SOUL OF A DEAL

MICHELLE PELUSO

SOMETIMES, A DISASTER IS JUST
A PAUSE IN THE GRAND PLAN

Michelle Peluso has had a meteoric career. Following her tenure at Boston Consulting Group, Michelle founded and served as CEO of travel company Site59, which she later sold to Travelocity. As I was writing this book, Michelle was named as the first ever chief marketing officer of IBM.

Generally speaking, when a big company (in this case Travelocity) buys a smaller company, the CEO and founder of the smaller company leaves the combined entity within one to two years. The kind of person who is willing to risk launching a startup from scratch and retains full control of that startup is typically not well suited for an "operational job." This is why entrepreneurs tend to have a hard time transitioning into executive roles that require reporting to a new CEO. But this was not Michelle's story. She went on to become the CEO of Travelocity, which included growing the company significantly and later taking it private.

After her time at Travelocity, Michelle spent several years as the global consumer chief marketing and digital officer at Citibank, working on the future of banking. She left to become the CEO of Gilt Group, one of the most successful e-commerce businesses today, and she is still in that role.

Our conversation focused on Michelle's time at Site59, its sale to Travelocity, and the story of how she eventually became that company's CEO.

Michelle founded Site59 in 1999 and was the company CEO. She built her company by hiring some of her closest friends. Site59 specialized in getting their customers killer deals on travel if they were willing to take a trip at the last minute. This was lucrative business for Site59, as well as for the airlines and hotels that would otherwise have had empty seats or rooms.

Site59 was the first in its industry to offer dynamic packaging by combining distressed airline inventory with distressed hotel inventory for weekend getaways. The airlines and the hotels were willing to provide discounts for these getaways because the actual price of the room or airfare was not transparent to any of Site59's customers. Site59's technology and strategy were successful and innovative, and the company did well from inception.

By 2001, Site59 had grown to about 80 employees and had strong financial backers such as Goldman Sachs and BCG. The company started getting several acquisition offers, mostly because the dynamic packaging idea was new and Site59 was the merchant of record for all of the hotel packages it put together. (At that time, being the merchant of record was becoming more and more important in the travel industry.)

Michelle met with her co-founders in August of 2001. They discussed the fact that while Site59 had experienced tremendous growth during the two years since its launch, they recognized it was going to be hard for the company to continue to be a stand-alone entity. They realized that either a big travel company would buy them out or they would have to build up Site59 themselves. Either way, the big players were coming into their space.

Site59 used a direct-to-consumer service business model in a market dominated by established players such as Travelocity, Orbitz, and Expedia. This made competition for customers much less cost-effective. For these reasons, they decided to entertain acquisition offers and find a good fit for the future of Site59.

By early September 2001, the company had received formal offer letters, some of which were quite compelling. Michelle spent much of the day on September 10th negotiating with Travelocity, the lead company in the pack, and felt they were getting pretty close to coming to terms on a deal. On September 11th, 2001, everything changed.

Site59 was truly a Ground Zero company. Their offices were just two blocks away from the Twin Towers, and they were working in the travel industry, which literally came to a screeching halt that fateful day. Michelle recalls, "I was walking to work, and I saw the gaping hole in one of the towers. I called our chief operating officer, who had just come out of the subway there. An American Airlines plane ticket had fluttered to her feet. This visual startled her, and when she saw it, she knew what had happened. The next couple of days were pure chaos. We had customers stranded all over the world. We lost our office for months. We had zero revenue in the days after. We called off all acquisition conversations because, at that point, we clearly went from a position of great strength to a position of total weakness."

As Michelle recounted to me, on so many levels, the disaster of 9/11 was hard for Site59 to deal with. "We were close to profitable with about $2M in the bank," she explained. "And all of a sudden, we were using up our cash savings quickly and had no revenue coming in. We really had to secure our investors, regain their confidence, and get them to put some money in the bank quickly, as we risked going out of business."

Michelle and her senior team also had to heal Site59's employees. "All of us saw things that day that we should never have seen," she explained. "So on the one hand, you're rebuilding the company, not letting this be the end of the story. Then, on the other hand, you're rebuilding morale. That was hugely emotionally charged and challenging, but also rallying, making us mission-driven for weeks and months."

Michelle thinks what saved the company was the fact that they were a very close team. Most of them had been friends for many years. They decided not to let the disaster of 9/11 break them. Over the next few months, as the country began to figure out its new normal, Michelle and her team decided to move fast. They took advantage of the fact that Site59 was small and nimble in the market, and got more hotels online. The good news for the company was that they started picking up growth right away. By February, they were back to the size they had been in August. By March, they were close to double that size—and profitable.

Around this time, Michelle started to consider the idea of selling the company again. Some of her reasons were the same, but she had some new reasons, too. Before 9/11, she and her team had been worried about the big players getting into the dynamic packaging game. Now, there was added pressure. That fall, the airlines had declared, "We're cutting commissions to zero." Now, all the major travel players had even more of an incentive to drive the merchant-modeled dynamic packaging, hotel-led businesses. One of the ways Site59 had catapulted back to growth was by powering those sections of their websites, so they knew that if they didn't figure out how to do hotel-led dynamic packaging better than anyone else, the market could be taken out from under them.

Michelle and her team decided to dive into getting a deal done with Travelocity. Site59's acquisition came about quickly because they had gotten so far down the path with Travelocity the first time and had remained on good terms with the management and owners of the company.

As Michelle recounted, "Travelocity was sort of the 'lead horse' before 9/11, so we felt like we had already done our homework and selected the company that best fit us." In addition, Expedia had their own hotel offering, Hotels.com, but Travelocity did not, so it really was a great fit. "Even from what Expedia's team could accomplish and their vision for the product, I think we felt that Travelocity had more need, was more air-dependent, had outsourced hotels, and were much more open to giving the team space to pursue bigger things."

While Michelle was trying to find the best home for her team with the most growth potential, she didn't think she would stay at the combined company for more than six months or so; she thought she would do the integration and then move on. Part of this had to do with relocation, as Travelocity was a Texas-based company, and Texas is a long way from New York. But as fate would have it, Travelocity became Michelle's home for the next eight years. Not only did she stay at Travelocity, but she also impressed the company's executive team and investors so much that within than two years, she was promoted to CEO.

When I asked Michelle to reflect on the success she'd achieved at Site59 and the company's acquisition by Travelocity, she said, "I think what worked about the Site59 experience was, 1) we didn't go into the business to sell the company, we went into the business to build a great business, and 2) we were really passionate about building something great, and I wanted to build a team that was great. But we didn't let that cloud our rational thinking when we started getting a bunch of calls [from potential buyers]." The second point is REALLY important, especially with so many Millennials starting companies with the singular focus of selling it to the highest bidder within a year or two. This is not how great companies are made. Great companies are made when the founding team is passionate about the business and focused on building a company that endures and is successful over the long-term.

Michelle continued: "The threat that we could disintegrate because bigger, richer players would invest in the industry we had pioneered was real. We didn't let our zeal and our passion overshadow rational thinking. [T]he cultural and strategic fit with Travelocity was just very strong."

"In retrospect," Michelle concluded, "when I think about deals I haven't done well, I realize that sometimes, you get so excited about getting a deal done that even though you know there's going to be social and cultural issues, you don't attack those issues head-on before you get the deal done. For example, addressing, 'Is it going to be your guy running this, or is it going to be our guy?' Or, one level below, 'Is it this or is it that? Are you going to go with this plan or are you going to have your own? Are we expecting you to really convert technology right away, or over time?' In particularly competitive processes, you can sometimes downplay the issues and feel like 'We'll deal with it after the fact.' In my experience, I've made mistakes there."

So many acquisitions and major projects fail not because of strategic rationale, but because of cultural issues or obstacles to realizing those projects' strategic value. When selling to Travelocity, Michelle spent a lot of time on those issues, especially some tricky ones, including whom she would report to. She had to think hard about that and have multiple conversations about it with the company's CEO.

Michelle had some great wisdom about the process of putting two companies together. "You spend an endless amount of time on the strategic rationale, what the gives and gets are going to be, what the biggest opportunities are for aligning, and seeing how this drives the synergy model. You spend an endless amount of time on exchange ratios and what each of them is worth and how you structure the deal. You spend inordinate amounts of time on legal issues and terms. It's remarkable to me how little time you generally spend on culture and HR. Most deals end up failing due to oversight of these oh-so-critical issues."

KEY POINTS IN THIS DEAL:

- Don't let your zeal or passion about your company overshadow rational financial analysis and risks.

- Sometimes, you have to be willing to say "no" to a deal, and sometimes a deal has to die and come back to the table more than once before it's consummated.

SORRY, I CAN'T TAKE ANY MORE OF YOUR MONEY

From early 2007 through mid-2014, I focused all of my professional energy on being an investor. During this time, I was an active angel investor through my investment company, Chance Technologies, in addition to being a venture partner for Accel Partners and the co-founder and managing director of Amplify.LA, the leading startup accelerator in Los Angeles.

While it may sound like I had three jobs, they were really one—investing, which I practiced through three different vehicles depending on the stage of a given investment opportunity. When a company was brand new and just getting off the ground, having raised either no money or a small "friends and family" round, investing with Amplify.LA generally made sense. When a company was in the process of raising a seed round (usually $500K-$2M), I would approach an investment opportunity as an angel investor with Chance. When a company was more advanced and raising their Series A of $5M or above, investing in them was typically an opportunity for Accel.

Being an investor can be extremely satisfying. It's financially rewarding to invest $100K and get back between $1M and several million dollars, and it's satisfying to mentor first-time CEOs through their own success, which you also get to participate in. But being an investor also has its downsides. It can be devastating when your $100K goes to zero, and it can be extremely frustrating when you share hard-earned experience with young founders and CEOs you've backed, and they don't take any of your advice.

In the first half of 2014, I was feeling more frustrated than rewarded in my work as an investor. Specifically, I felt that I was doing none of the fun stuff, while the people in whom I was investing were having a great time building successful companies and amazing products. So, around this time, I decided to find a company I could become the CEO of—either a company I started from scratch or a new company that was open to hiring an experienced CEO.

This decision changed the face of some of my meetings. Before it, I had only taken meetings that made sense for me as an investor. Now, I wanted to learn about every startup in LA to see if they might be a good fit for me as a CEO. In addition, I had regular meetings with a few of the smartest people I had worked with in the past to explore our own ideas and to see if anything bubbled up to the surface.

Two of these people were Minah Oh and Sascha Linn, both of whom had worked for me back when I was president of Disney Online and both of whom I had hired numerous times since to work for various companies I had consulted to or invested in. The three of us first started talking about product/company ideas during the early summer of 2014.

People often say "necessity is the mother of invention," and if you are trying to build a business, start by solving a problem that you have yourself. These thoughts led us to start talking about just how shitty the current options were for getting technical support for new technology. Sure, there is the Genius Bar at Apple if you're willing to make an appointment in advance and take your machine in. And then there's Geek Squad, which no one seems to like, but everyone seems to feels is a necessary evil. But beyond those options, we thought, where is the average person to go?

Even more puzzling to us was where the average person's parents were supposed to go (parents being people in their 50s and older). When this came up, we all kind of looked at each other and laughed, realizing that:

a)   We were the technical support provider for our parents and some friends/neighbors.

b)   We would rather pay to have someone provide technical support for our parents than do it ourselves.

c)   We believed that over the next few years, there would be an explosion of smart home devices, and with that explosion, an even larger need for in-home support.

d)   There was no good service to turn to.

These realizations were the beginning of our "aha" moment. We started doing research on consumer technical support. We guessed that Geek Squad probably did a few hundred million in revenue, and that the consumer technical support market was a few billion. What we discovered next surprised and excited us. Geek Squad did a reported $3B in revenue/year, and the consumer technical support market was about $20B/year. (That's billion with a B!) In addition, other than Geek Squad, there were no meaningful players in the industry, which meant that there were thousands of companies doing small, decent business every year, but no one was generating revenue like Geek Squad's.

Upon researching the details of Geek Squad, we became more and more intrigued. We learned that the $3B represented less than 10% of the revenue of the entire BestBuy chain but approximately half of its profit. This meant that the tech support business is more profitable than the retail business. (This isn't too surprising when you realize that in order to stay relevant, BestBuy and other retailers match in-store prices with Amazon and other web-based competitors. This means that on a $1000 television, Best Buy probably makes $40-$50 bucks.)

During the late summer 2014, armed with this data, we officially set out to define a business that would enter and disrupt the consumer tech support industry and the budding smart home category. Our plan was straightforward: If we could offer better support than Geek Squad, including faster turnaround times and lower prices, then we would have a solid business opportunity in a $20B and growing market. It was simple enough. But how could we cost-effectively recruit and train talented technicians, how would we get the word out that we existed, and how could we offer our service for less than our competitors did?

Uber was one of the first companies to capitalize on and succeed in a two-sided marketplace in a large industry that was ripe for disruption: on-demand car service/taxis. For the most part, before Uber, if you wanted on-demand car service to the airport or a meeting, you had to arrange this through a company that had a fleet of Lincoln Town Cars and full-time drivers. As a result, the cost of such on-demand car services were pretty high and out of reach for most people. Uber, however, especially with their UberX service, which allowed anyone with a halfway decent car to become an UberX driver, totally disrupted the on-demand car space and in doing so, provided as good or better service at a much lower rate. This was a win-win for everyone except the taxi and high-end car service companies, which were devastated. At the time this was being written, many of them were lobbying for legislation that would shut Uber down.

2014 was the year of "the Uber for X." Our initial idea for our IT startup was called "Uber for In-Home Tech Support," but the challenge of how would we find a large and on-demand technical talent base seemed daunting. We needed to figure out how would we train them and test their skills.

Things really came together when we realized that most college students are the technical support providers for their parents and older family friends. Today's college-aged kids only know a world with with wireless and mobile Internet access—a world that is more comfortable on mobile devices and tablets than traditional PCs. They have grown up with technology at the center of their world. Essentially, they're "UberX drivers for computers." They have the skills, they have the time (and can control when they are on or off the clock), and they are willing to work for a lot less money than what the Geek Squad charges its customers ($99 initiation fee and another $99/hour).

Armed with this information, Minah, Sascha, and I began to have weekly meetings to discuss our ideas about how we would roll out our service, what technology we would need to build, how we saw the business scaling, and where we saw the business going over the course of two to five-plus years. While the basic idea was exciting enough, it really hit a stride when we realized that today's retail stores—especially for new technologies—are dinosaurs that are destined to become extinct. However, new technologies for the home are being released at an accelerating rate, so how will consumers learn about and get new technology installed in the home as quickly as it comes out? The answer was exciting: through our extended, student-based workforce!

The students would come to us with a base level of understanding of how to support PCs running Windows, Macintoshes, wireless networks, smartphones, and iPads. We would hone those skills with some technical testing before they were allowed to go out on calls, but we would also expose them to the latest, best, newest technology for the home. Our workers would also inform customers of special offers to get the latest and greatest in tech.

Examples of this included the Nest Thermostat, which was recently bought by Google for $2B, the wireless audio music system by Sonos, and the advanced TV platform by Roku. In particular, we identified our audience—those in their 50s and over—as awesome potential customers because they are interested in new technology but don't know enough about the latest and greatest. They also have money to spend to get the new gadgets and pay for support, and they would feel good about helping students pay their way through college.

In the next phase, we decided to double down on colleges. Here, we would seek out not only technical talent but also our first trial customers by going to alumni associations and explaining we had a better mousetrap for technical support. We came up with a very specific plan wherein we would "Alpha" test the idea by hiring UCLA students (my alma mater) and marketing to a five to ten mile radius around UCLA, which is a very affluent area.

By October 2014, we had decided to raise some venture capital funding to get this company off the ground. I was hopeful that the funding would come together by the end of the year so that we could hit the ground running on the first of 2015. But with venture, you never know. Given my longtime relationship with them, my first stop was Accel Partners. Right away, they told me they were interested. I told them I wanted to raise $2M on a $7M valuation, but that I only wanted $500K from them. I wanted proof of support from other venture capital firms. Specifically, I wanted some LA-based firms to be in the round.

The capital structure is where the soul really came in: telling Accel I wanted them, but only for $500K, and that I planned to seek funding from other firms in LA. All this had to be done before Thanksgiving because the venture capital world basically shuts down between Thanksgiving and New Year's.

Accel took the deal. And with my $500K from them secured, I chose two other LA-based firms I wanted to invest at the same level. One was Upfront Ventures, the largest VC firm in LA. The other was more of a boutique firm called CrossCut Ventures. I knew all of the the partners at these firms personally, and I knew how involved they could get with the businesses they invested in. This made them very attractive investors for our company.

Things couldn't have gone better. Within two weeks, I had Accel at $500K, Upfront at $500K, CrossCut at $500K, Amplify.LA at $250K and some of the best angel investors in Los Angeles coming in at between $50K and $100K. Now, the problem was that I was, as they say in the VC industry, "oversubscribed." I had wanted to raise only $2M, and I had commitments for well over that amount. I discussed this with my team and our primary investors, and we agreed we would raise as much as $2.5M, but not a dollar more. That's when things got kind of wacky.

A local LA staple called ideaLab!, which has spawned some of the city's best companies, told me they really wanted to invest and asked how much they could put in. I told them there was only $50K available, and taking even that would require that I cut some of the angels back. Then, another Los Angeles-based VC firm, BasePoint Ventures, offered to invest. Again, I told them I could take no more than $50K. I cut all my investors back a little (other than the primary three), and told ideaLab! and BasePoint I needed signed docs and funding by the following Monday, or I would give their allocations to someone else.

Make no mistake, this is a dream scenario in getting a company off the ground, and it is certainly not the norm. In retrospect, I think it was a due to a combination of my past successes, the fact that the entire senior founding team had worked together on and off for 20 years (which removed a lot of risk), and that we had a very good idea at a very good time.

I worked with the investors systematically, choosing who to get a "yes" from first, then going to people I knew would be positively influenced by that first "yes" and giving them an aggressive but realistic deadline to get their funding in. This process was the "Soul of Fund Raising" for our Uber-modeled in-home tech support service, which we decided to call HelloTech, and it worked amazingly well. Now, about two and a half years into the life of HelloTech, we are beginning to see our vision come to fruition.

We loved hiring college students, but I worried that a nationwide city-by-city recruiting effort would take us two to three years. We needed to have a national presence to secure big national deals to be the installation, support, and/or training partner for consumer electronics companies, smart home companies, and more.

In middle of 2016, we decided to acquire a company called Geekatoo. In business for over five years, Geekatoo had amassed a nationwide network of over 6,000 technicians. In Geekatoo, we found the solution to our problem of building up a national presence. But the question was how we could acquire them in a cost-effective manner.

Fortunately for us, the three creators of Geekatoo were first-time founders and had had trouble raising real funding for their business. By the end of 2015, just a little over a year since the formation of HelloTech, we had raised $13M in venture capital, including a Series A round of $9.5M lead by Madrona Ventures in Seattle. Geekatoo, on the other hand, had raised only $2.7M in their five-year history.

When we approached Geekatoo, they were tired and weary of running the company on a month-to-month basis, trying to squeeze a little profit to pay the bills. Our timing was perfect. We offered Geekatoo 28% of our company in stock for the merger of the two companies with a one-time cash payment of $900K to the three co-founders.

Buying Geekatoo was absolutely the right thing to do. And as of this writing, HelloTech is fast becoming the in-home installation, training, and support partner for such electronics makers and smart home companies as Samsung, Ring, AARP, Altice, and Luma who are looking to benefit from an "on-demand, lower-priced Geek Squad" without having to build or manage it themselves.

KEY POINTS IN THIS DEAL:

- When raising money, go for your dream team. Don't worry too much about whether you might offend someone by not letting them invest their desired full amount.

- When trying to get multiple partners on board, remember that landing the biggest partner first will help you get the others to follow suit.

- Investors, like people in general, tend to want the thing they can't have more than they want the thing they can easily obtain. The "impression of scarcity" in deal making is an art form to study and learn.

CHAPTER 8
STICKING TO YOUR BELIEFS

MARIA EITEL

LET'S HEAR IT FOR THE GIRLS

I am fortunate to count Maria Eitel as a friend. Maria is a power-house—always full of positive energy, enthusiasm, and a can-do attitude. She is the founding president of the Nike Foundation, which was formed in 2004, and she is the force behind the Nike-funded creative social business "Girl Effect." Since 2015, Girl Effect has been a global force working, as its website describes, "with girls and those around them to create active champions of a world in which she reaches her full potential and the cycle of poverty is disrupted."[7]

Bloomberg, BusinessWeek, Forbes, and the *New York Times* have all noted Girl Effect's powerful message about how investing in ado-lescent girls can transform a country's economic development. And

---

7   Source: GirlEffect.org, http://www.girleffect.org/our-purpose/.

data bears this message out. Take India, for example. The World Bank has calculated that each year, the country's nearly four million adolescent new mothers cost India $383B in potential lifetime income. The Nike Foundation and its partners have invested more than $250M to support Girl Effect's efforts to help impoverished young women across the globe overcome barriers including poor access to education and adolescent motherhood to reach their full potential.

Maria and I sat down to discuss the very early days of the Nike Foundation and how she was able to form Girl Effect through a masterful and maniacal focus on deals and partnerships.

In 2004, when Maria and Nike set out to establish Girl Effect, they intentionally zeroed in girls, not women. As Maria pointed out, this is a very important distinction. While women's causes are certainly important, as Maria shared, less than ½ of each cent of humanitarian aid is earmarked for girls. This is why Girl Effect has focused specifically on adolescent girls, who are at a particularly important crossroads in their lives.

In 2006, Maria and the Nike Foundation produced an impactful paper together with the World Bank. It concerned the theory that delaying the birth of a first child has a positive material impact on the mother's life and the community she lives in. Even with this progress and information, raising initial awareness for Girl Effect proved more challenging than Maria anticipated.

As fate would have it, Maria attended an advisory committee meeting for the World Bank and found herself sitting next to Mark Lowcock, the managing director for the Department for International Development (DFID), a governmental organization in the United Kingdom. This encounter proved to be very serendipitous for both

Maria and Mark. During the event, the two lamented how difficult it was to achieve the scale of attention necessary to drive resources to girls and women in need. At that time, girls' and women's issues were a sidebar; around the world, these did not figure into government or NGO agendas or budgets. Maria told me that throughout the day, she and Mark each said, "You've got to be kidding me. It shouldn't be this difficult to get important and transformative support programs financed for girls and women."

Maria seized the opportunity that meeting with Mark afforded her. After the conference, they began a relationship that helped them show the World Bank and the world more generally that they were simply not doing enough for girls. Maria made sure she and Mark had proof points from the World Bank study to back up their claims, and she and Mark developed a plan for their organizations to tackle the issues together and address challenges in a way that would really make a difference. In Mark, Maria had found a partner who would treat the hurdles adolescent girls faced as seriously as she did.

Maria, Mark, and their teams from the Nike Foundation and DFID began working together on constructing a program. Through their early work, they learned that their two organizations couldn't have been more different. Nike was a creative, shoot-from-the-hip, U.S. company and brand that could turn on a dime (compared to most corporations). The British government, on the other hand, was just that—an entire governmental body with a tremendous amount of bureaucracy that was accustomed to working very slowly. It preferred to organize commissions to conduct years of research before committing to a program.

However, Maria and Mark were undaunted by the differences in their organizations. Instead, they were united by a common goal and true desire to change the lives of millions of girls worldwide. They committed to act as champions for their respective organizations and develop a "true partnership" that would have real and measurable impact. When they said "partnership," they meant it—down to planning and implementing their programs. They reassured each other that theirs would not be a hands-off partnership, where each entity simply did its own thing and called it collaboration. They were both motivated and driven by the question: "What if we had a real partnership and worked together in a deep way?"

Over the next eighteen months, Mark and Maria worked side-by-side to design, conceptualize, and co-fund a true partnership deal. It was no easy task. They faced challenges at every turn, particularly the differences in their cultures and the timelines the two entities were accustomed to working under. It was only as a result of Maria and Mark's commitment and maniacal focus that their partnership deal worked. Their dedication was the "soul" of the deal.

In recounting the deal, Maria told me there were many times during the 18-month planning cycle that either team could have given up. Keeping the collaboration alive was an act of sheer will, creativity, persistence, and passion on Maria and Mark's parts. Finding a way for the teams to work together required consistent leadership. But the Nike Foundation and DFID had agreed on the goal, objective, and vision of the partnership. They were focused on improving the lives of girls all over the world.

In the end, both organizations moved quite outside their normal operating procedures to understand and work with each other. Nike became more data-oriented, while DFID became more creative. Creativity was even required to determine what each party could bring to the table. Together, they designed the precursor to Girl Effect. It was called "Girl Hub."

Like all deals, the consummation was not the end of the partnership, but merely the beginning. Once signed, the partners worked closely together over the next year (while continuing to adapt to the other's styles and strengths) to design the program and select the countries where it would initially be launched. Even though they knew early on that each side needed to have empathy for the other and understand its traditional workings, it wasn't until midway through that first year that they had to face a significant truth: Before they could deploy the program, they needed to meld their cultures.

The melding of cultures is a trick in and of itself. In the case of Nike and DFID, the organizations found that culture worked its way all the way down to little things, such as each entity's understanding of words like "success," "measurement," and "due diligence." These words were important to each organization and the joint program itself, so coalescing their divergent definitions was critical to their ability to jointly deploy a successful program.

As Maria explained, she had an "aha" moment when she realized that, as different as they were, each organization was great in its own way. She needed to embrace and appreciate their differences in order for everyone to succeed. At the beginning, things couldn't have been more dissimilar for the two groups, but in the end, they developed an appreciation and respect for each other. Soon, Girl Hub went to work with an annual budget of approximately $25M, focusing primarily on Ethiopia, Nigeria, and Rwanda.

Maria said she felt the partnership really hit its stride and achieved what so many had doubted they could when UK Prime

Minister David Cameron spoke publically about the importance of the Girl Hub in June 2014. He was in attendance at the group's first ever meet up, "Girl Summit"—a collaboration between Girl Hub, DFID, and other major partners.

In 2015, Girl Hub became Girl Effect. And as of 2017, the organization has progressed beyond Maria and Mark's original vision, building on its successes and expanding its efforts to bring education and resources to young women around the globe.

In closing, Maria shared some key aspects of this groundbreaking deal she believes are relevant to any complex transaction.

KEY POINTS IN THIS DEAL:

- Clear, shared goals that keep the teams focused on the right things when the going gets rough.

- Not being afraid to be maniacal: Don't to take "no" for an answer and make sure leadership is exhibited from both sides of the table.

- Finding the passion necessary to work through the inevitable bumps in the road.

- Motivating deal teams in such a way that both parties become irrationally committed to getting the deal done.

- Connecting to peoples' emotional reasons for wanting to consummate a deal. Getting deals done is hard, and emotions help tilt the scales in your favor.

(Ask deal teams, "How will you feel better about yourself if we complete this deal?")

- Getting creative with the other side to understand their objectives and walk away points. (Another case where empathy matters.)

And last but not least, hard work!

WHITNEY JOHNSON

THE SOUL OF A STOCK

Sometimes, you get lucky when you reach out to people you don't know for help. You may find someone who is generous with both their time and their knowledge. This was the case when I reached out to Whitney Johnson via Twitter. I was familiar with her work and her then almost-published book, *Disrupt Yourself*. I shared my vision for this book with her and asked if she would be so kind as to let me interview her. She obliged, even in the midst of working on her own book and running her business.

Whitney is a powerhouse. She was also a finalist for the "Top Thinkers on Talent" at the biennial Thinkers50 Ceremony in London. She is best known for her work on driving corporate innovation through personal disruption. Alongside Clayton Christiansen, Whitney is the co-founder of Rose Park Advisors. Together, they led the $8M seed round for Korea's Coupang (originally the Groupon of Korea, and now the Amazon of Korea), which is currently valued at $5B+. Having served as president of Rose Park Advisors from 2007-2012, Whitney was involved in the fund's formation, raising capital, and developing the fund's strategy.

When our interview began, Whitney had a strong idea about what she wanted to share with me. She felt her background made her better suited to address the "soul of a stock" instead of the "soul of a deal." Her input was not only compelling but also completely unique and a perfect addition to the messages and lessons I have chosen to share in this book.

Whitney shared with me her history as an equity analyst covering the telecom and media sector with a focus on Latin America. Early on, she covered Televisa, which as she described the ABC/CBS/NBC/ Fox of Mexico all rolled into one. Her original opinion of Televisa was quite negative. She observed that the company was saddled with debt needed a turnaround, and she downgraded the stock.

Analysts downgrade stocks all the time. But Univision brought Whitney's report into a Televisa board meeting, which put the management under tremendous scrutiny. They took the downgrade personally, and in their own way, they retaliated against Whitney. Shortly after the report, she participated—or attempted to participate—in the Televisa earnings call. All her questions and comments were blatantly ignored, which was highly unusual.

Similar to my thesis that deals have souls, Whitney explained to me why stock prices also have a soul. Stock prices are generally about momentum and reflect current events at a company. They are susceptible to whatever narrative management is trying to write and whether or not investors buy into that story. If the narrative does not resonate, the "soul of the stock" is negatively impacted, and the price suffers.

Whitney strongly held that Televisa needed a turnaround. She did not subscribe to its senior management's narrative, so she went out on a limb and downgraded the stock. However, as a professional, Whitney continued to evaluate the stock over time, closely watching the actions of the company. A new CEO who was trying to take the company out of the shadow of his father and make it his own had initiated actions she believed would turn Televisa around. For example, he started selling off non-strategic assets in an effort get out from under the debt that initially led her to downgrade the company's stock. The sale of the assets and the reduction of debt, along with overall increased return on investment, allowed her to change her rating and upgrade Televisa to a buy.

When Whitney upgraded the stock, some of the bigger mutual funds, including Fidelity, confronted her regarding her change of heart. She responded with her observation that the new CEO was taking bold steps to turn the company around, reduce debt, and increase ROI. While it was a change in rating, she explained, she knew the upgrade was the right action to take.

Whitney discussed with me how this sort of transformation shows that stocks have a soul and that this soul can change over time, just as the process of closing a deal can change over time based on its dynamic nature. In Televisa's case, Whitney witnessed a generational transition that allowed her to downgrade the stock when appropriate and then upgrade it according to the same principle. For her, paying attention to trends within the company and in its sector gave her a sense of the stock's direction (and soul), which helped her make the appropriate calls.

Another example of the soul of a stock was America Movil, the largest mobile phone company in Mexico. Whitney began coverage in 2002, when mobile penetration was about 15% but already greater than wire line penetration. (In many countries, wire lines were completely skipped and immediately supplanted by wireless.) Whitney felt strongly that the Mexican mobile market could to grow beyond the 15% penetration, so she instituted a buy recommendation on the stock. This was questioned by many in the space. However, the ensuing growth outpaced even Whitney's prediction—wireless would eventually reach 40% penetration.

Within a few years, America Movil became the fourth largest cellular provider in the world. Today, 90% of the Mexican market has wireless service, which has far outpaced the country's wire line offerings. America Movil was one of Whitney's more successful picks. She believes that looking into the soul of the market in Mexico allowed her to predict that the stock would experience astronomical growth. Years later, people still come up to her and thank her for the rating. They say they made a fortune following her advice.

Whitney explained that whether she was downgrading or upgrading, someone was always upset with her. The lesson is that there are always two parties evaluating any stock she may rate: one on the buy side, and one on the sell side. As such, she learned to pay attention to the narrative of the company she was rating—to search for the soul of the story behind the stock and stick with her conviction regarding what it was going to do, even if people on her own team questioned her or others were downright upset with her. She learned that sometimes, in order to get the best outcome, one has to be willing to go out on a ledge, even if it upsets some very powerful people.

KEY POINTS IN THIS DEAL:

- It's okay to change your mind on a deal if the fundamental aspects of the business change over time.

- Sometimes, you have to be willing to be unpopular in order to do the right thing for a deal.

DR. DAMBISA MOYO

HEY, WOULD YOU MIND GRABBING
AN APPLE WATCH?

I met Dambisa through our mutual involvement in a nonprofit organization. She is an incredibly accomplished person with an international pedigree beyond that of anyone else I've ever met. Her contribution adds some valuable international deal-making expertise to this book.

Dr. Dambisa Moyo, a native of Zambia, is a global economist who analyzes global macroeconomics and international affairs. She advises companies, corporate boards, CEOs, and management teams on investment decisions, capital allocation, and risk management. Dambisa serves on the boards of Barclays Bank, the financial services group; Barrick Gold, the global miner; SABMiller, the global brewer; and Seagate Technology. Her work has taken her to nearly 80 countries over the last decade, during which time she has developed a unique knowledge of the inherent conflicts facing developed economies as well as the interaction between politics, international finance, and global markets.

For our conversation, Dambisa thought it would be useful to explain some of the nuances of working in international business in general rather than focusing on one specific deal. I wasn't going to argue with her about what would be most interesting.

Dambisa began by mentioning the hubris Americans often have—that we believe we know what is best. From Dambisa's perspective, many Americans tend to believe they know what companies are best, what deals are best, the best way to finance deals, and the best way to negotiate and close deals. In her experience working in nearly 80 countries, she feels we often underestimate or misinterpret our international counterparts, usually because they are not entirely fluent in our language or our ways of doing business. As a result, we miss out on good deals.

One of the key tenets of deal making Dambisa has learned, especially in her international work, is that it's much better to listen than to speak. She explained that this approach runs counter to arguments presented in American textbooks on deal making, which encourage assertiveness and collaboration. However, when in another country and unfamiliar with local customs or ways of doing business, far more damage than good can be done if you speak before taking the time to understand the mindset of the people with whom you are meeting.

Dambisa also finds that Americans often assume we are more sophisticated or better traveled than the people we encounter in our meetings. We assume that just because the other party is not perfectly fluent in English, they don't know how to value a company. We don't ask ourselves, "What must be true for them to be willing to pay this premium for this asset?" In many cases, we assume we are more in the know than they are, and we fail to consider our own lack of understanding. Perhaps we are the less sophisticated ones at the table.

During our conversation, Dambisa specifically pinpointed mining as an industry where these tendencies are prevalent. (She is an expert on the industry.) Sometimes, Dambisa has found, one party's approach to determining the value of a mine takes more into account than Excel spreadsheets or cash flow data than the other's. Therefore, what may seem to one person like an overpayment will not seem this way to a person who understands the buyer's valuation methods.

Dambisa argued that the U.S. way of doing business is actually the non-standard way when compared with the rest of the world's and that this puts Americans at a disadvantage when it comes to working on international business deals. Americans falsely assume that rest of the world is similar to them rather than different. When American business professionals go overseas to do deals, we tend not to understand or even pay attention to our counterparts' standards for business relationships.

One big difference between American standards and others is that is in the U.S., businesspeople tend to do deals during business hours in business settings (with the exception of the golf course). However, in the rest of the world, business does not stop at 5 p.m. In fact, it often starts after 5 p.m. in a relaxed bar setting or another after-hours venue. As Dambisa explained, "There is a civility around doing business as an extension of cultural life, not just in the office." She emphasized that most of the world sees the U.S. as the least enjoyable country to do business with.

Another point of contention concerns the subtleties between culturally and/or ethically acceptable practices in other countries versus in the U.S. In the U.S., we think we have a strong sense of what it means to deal with bribery or corruption. So much so, in fact, that the SEC created the Foreign Corrupt Practices Act in 1977.[8] But when working with foreign countries, the distinct lines of corruption can be harder to discern than an American may think.

Dambisa shared an example with me. She was about to leave New York for a foreign country where she planned to obtain a license to do trade and operate a mine. As she was leaving, she received a

---

8   For more on the Foreign Corrupt Practices Act, see: https://www.sec.gov/spotlight/foreign-corrupt-practices-act.shtml.

call from a staff member from that country's Minister of Trade. Very casually, he asked, "Would you mind picking up an Apple Watch on your way here? They are not available in this country yet, and we will reimburse you."

This seemed like an innocent enough request. It was an item valued at several hundred dollars, not tens or hundreds of thousands, and the Ministry of Trade had promised to reimburse Dambisa. When she arrived at the first meeting in the country, she handed the watch to the Minister and said his staff had asked if she would be so kind as to bring it with her. He graciously accepted the watch. The meeting extended into after-business hours, drinks became involved, and everything went well. As the meeting came to an end, nobody made mention of reimbursing Dambisa for the watch. What should she do? By the strictest of standards, even just a few hundred bucks could be deemed a bribe. But asking for reimbursement could insult the Minister or his staff and jeopardize a significant business transaction.

Dambisa told me that in such situations (which she works to avoid whenever possible), her overarching rule is that humanity drives the decision. If there is no black and white line, Dambisa counsels, you must put yourself in the mindset of your counterparts. When dealing with poorer countries in particular, it is important to know that small gifts and gestures matter. It's easy to carry a watch or an iPhone to a country where they can't get those products.

Dambisa's best workaround is to establish relationships with potential international counterparts before she is in the middle of a deal. These relationships are often formed over a long period of time during which the two parties build an understanding that prevents these kinds of situations from happening. It is much easier to explain at the beginning of a relationship that bringing gifts is against your company policy than it is to explain this down the road, when you're en route to consummating a business transaction.

It has been through building meaningful relationships over time that Dambisa has been so successful in her work all over the world. This is a real investment beyond what most U.S. business people are accustomed to. For example, when she visits people in other countries, it is common for her to discover they have taken the time to find learn about her background and personal life. Often, they know that she runs marathons, for example, and that she likes to play tennis. They've taken an extra step to find out what she's interested in.

In the U.S., Dambisa feels, we are too focused on placing a dollar value on our time, which makes us not nearly as good at investing in relationships that can last years and span generations. She observed that Americans understand the 30,000-foot view but not the ground-level perspective needed to operate in other countries. We may punch a clock in the U.S. between business and leisure, but for the rest of the world, the line between the end of the business day and the beginning of social life is blurry.

KEY POINTS TO DAMBISA'S INSIGHT:

- Don't assume third world countries' business and political leaders do not comprehend American culture simply because they're not fluent in English.

- Be willing to turn the other cheek on minor issues such as trade/gifts that are acceptable and common aspects of doing business in other countries.

- The rest of the world doesn't have a hard line between business and social times of day.

- It is often better to listen than to speak, especially early on in a deal.

SO, NOW YOU WANT TO
HELP THE SICK KIDS???

During my pre-teen years and early adolescence, I regularly got very sick. There seemed to be a pattern. I would wake up in the morning feeling fine, but by midday, I would have flu-like symptoms. By evening, I would have a temperature, sometimes as high as 104 degrees.

After years of my symptoms worsening, my doctors decided to put me through a barrage of x-rays and tests. This went on for almost a year. It's all somewhat of a blur, but I remember missing quite a bit of school and spending many days at the doctor's office or the hospital. Eventually, they did a "lower GI," which is effectively a live X-ray of your colon. The results of that test were conclusive; I was diagnosed with Crohn's disease. I was 14 years old and had just started high school.

Part of me must have been scared. But I think a bigger part of me was simply happy to have an answer. It took so long to land on a diagnosis because I hadn't shown the normal signs of Crohn's disease, which are typically really bad gut cramps. Adding to this, there was also limited awareness of Crohn's disease at the time as well as limited treatment information.

The next five years were very physically challenging for me. As the disease progressed, the cramps began and then became worse and worse. For the better part of that time, I was on prednisone, a steroid, which made me gain a lot of weight and look bloated. During those years, my cramps and condition were bad enough that I needed to be hospitalized several times. When there was a blockage in my intestines, I needed to go on a clear liquid diet for a few days to allow them to calm down.

All through this time, I tried to be as normal as I could. For the most part, I hid my disease from my friends and classmates. They knew something was wrong because I missed so much school, but I simply wasn't comfortable sharing any information about my condition. It's hard enough being a teenager without suffering from a disease.

Despite all of the steroids I took during those five years, I was in pain on a daily basis. I never went anywhere without knowing where the closest bathroom was because when I needed it, I needed it right then! Today, they don't administer prednisone for prolonged periods of time because it wreaks havoc on the body. It also stunts your growth. (I would like to think I'd be over 6' tall rather than 5'9" if I hadn't taken all of those steroids.)

After five years of massive pharmacological treatment, I went to my doctors and begged they do something more. I couldn't bear the pain anymore. The doctor explained that the only other option was to have surgery to remove the affected intestines. He cautioned me that while surgery might fix the current problems, Crohn's has no cure and would likely affect the new part of my intestines in due time. I understood what he was saying, but I couldn't take it anymore. I was 5'8" and weighed about 90 pounds because I simply couldn't eat or process food. I opted for the surgery.

Preparing for the surgery was pretty intense. I was 19 years old and responsible for signing all of my own paperwork. Fortunately, I was still covered by my parents' health insurance, so that took a lot of the stress off. The night before the surgery, my doctors performed a series of x-rays to locate the most affected areas and determine where to cut me open. They explained they would make a 3"-4" horizontal incision across my abdomen, remove the affected areas, and connect all of the cut pieces of intestine back together. I would be in the hospital for between four and seven days and on a clear liquid diet for the first three to four of those, so that my intestines could have a chance to heal.

When the anesthesiologist came in and gave me the disclaimer about being put under (i.e., "there is a small chance that something could go wrong and you could die, now, please sign here"), it stopped me in my tracks for a minute. I would say that experience was my first real brush with mortality.

When I woke up from the surgery, I knew something had gone wrong. I was in a lot of pain, and it felt like the pain went from one side of my abdomen to the other. I asked the nurses tending to me what had happened, and they told me I would need to talk to the doctor when he came by for rounds. My parents didn't have any information, either.

When Dr. Funkelsrude (how could I forget a name like that?) came in to see me, I asked what the hell had happened. He explained that they opened a 4"-5" area of my abdomen on the left side. The affected areas were so spread out, however, that they needed to cut me open on the right side as well. He said he was surprised I had been able to survive as well as I had, given the extent of the damage. The surgeons had removed almost my entire colon and sigmoid colon, which connects the small intestine to the colon. While the surgery was extensive, the doctor said he thought I'd feel much better once my wounds healed.

For the next three days, I lay in the hospital bed sucking on ice chips. No food. No beverages. It was all part of the process of allowing the intestines to heal and grow back together. I remember so vividly the first meal I was allowed to have on day four: Cream of Wheat. As a result, Cream of Wheat is one of my favorite things to eat to this day!

One positive thing that came out of my hospital stay was meeting my roommates, who also had Crohn's disease and had also been in for fairly serious surgeries. For the first time in my life, I met people who had gone through the same pain and agony I had. It was so refreshing to be able to share openly with my newfound fast friends.

I am one of the fortunate ones. While I still have Crohn's disease (there is still no cure, but the treatment is far better), I have been able to manage my disease with diet. My gut cramps are worse than the average person's, but I haven't had any additional surgeries. I've been hospitalized only four to five times during the last 30 years. A lot of Crohn's sufferers are not as lucky; many need repeated surgeries.

In extreme cases, a patient's small intestines are removed, and the patient can become malnourished (the small intestines' job is to reclaim nutrients from the food you eat). Without some or all of its small intestine, the body cannot nourish itself by eating, only by hooking up to an IV every night. In very extreme cases, Crohn's can be a death sentence. One of the fast friends I met while recovering from my major surgery was David Kraft. At that time, he had already endured several surgeries. I kept in touch with him, and I knew his Crohn's was relentless. Ultimately, David succumbed to the illness, passing away at the age of 35. Needless to say, Crohn's has played a major role in my life and the life of everyone else who has it.

About a decade and a half after my surgery, I was 36 years old and had been newly hired by Disney as an "entertainment executive." I was approached by an organization called the Crohn's and Colitis Foundation (CCFA). (Colitis is a sister disease to Crohn's that affects only the colon, never the small intestine.) CCFA explained that their mission was to better educate those living with the disease along with their family and friends, and work toward better medical treatment and, ideally, a cure. I was asked to join the board of directors of the Los Angeles Chapter of the CCFA, and I told them I would do so under one condition—that all of my efforts were going to be focused on helping teens deal with the disease.

Little did I know at the time that when a nonprofit association asks you to join its board, they are essentially asking you to donate to their organization. I was okay with this arrangement—as long as the money I donated went toward helping teens deal with the disease.

During the next few years, I became more and more involved with the CCFA. Ultimately, I became the president of the Los Angeles chapter, and we held monthly meetings at my office.

A few years into my involvement with CCFA, I decided that my personal mission was to start a camp for teens with Crohn's and colitis so they could meet other kids going through the same thing. I wanted teen sufferers to feel comfortable enough to share intimate stories and advice, and to simply feel like they belonged. I pitched the idea to the national chapter of the CCFA and was both surprised and annoyed by the response: "Richard," they said. "What a great idea. We don't have any funds to do this, but if you donate or raise the funds necessary to open a camp, we will support it." WTF? I thought. Why wasn't this worthy of the funds that were already being raised? I pressed, but I got nowhere. The money that was being raised was already accounted for. Thus, I started down my path to begin Camp Oasis CCFA.

Between myself and some very generous friends, we put together the $25K it took to pay for a camp in Malibu. (We licensed a week-long stretch at an existing camp.) But the logistics were complicated. We needed a doctor and a nurse on site 24/7. We needed waivers from all of the parents stating that we had the right to perform medical treatment if necessary. We had to get the camp to alter their menu to accommodate people who suffered from Crohn's and colitis (read: less fiber). We also needed to help parents be comfortable with the idea of letting their sick child spend a week in Malibu without them.

Even with all these stipulations and challenges, we pulled it off. The first summer, we had only 15 to 20 kids, but the experience was magical and transformational for all involved.

Over the next few years, the camp grew steadily; first to 30 kids, then to 50. Each year it got better and better. All of the kids that attended came back in subsequent years. I couldn't have been more proud to see teens ranging from 13 to 17 years old, all sharing intimate stories and feeling so at peace.

Each year, the costs went up, and each year, I made the commitment to "give or get" (a phrase used in charities where you either GIVE them the money yourself or GET others to give) enough money to fund the camp. Fortunately, by the fourth year of operation, the camp began to get some press and recognition. As a result, it was easier to raise the money required to run the camp, even with rising costs. At that point, it cost roughly $1,200 to send one kid to camp for the week. (At the outset, we had made a commitment that families would have to pay only a $50 registration fee. We didn't want kids whose parents couldn't afford the camp to miss out.)

After several years, Camp Oasis finally generated more funds than it cost to run it. I remember the year very well. As I recall it, camp cost about $60,000 to run, and we raised about $80,000. It was a huge milestone. Even better, it put us $20K ahead for the next year. Or so I thought.

Just when we were ahead, things went off the rails. At the end of camp that summer, we had a meeting with the entire board and CCFA staff. I reported on the success for the year and announced we had a head start on the next. Then, the executive director of the CCFA in LA at the time (name withheld by my choice) said he thought it was time for the CCFA office to take responsibility for the finances of the camp.

At first, I was confused. But only for a minute. This bureaucratic weasel was trying to co-opt the $20K surplus and use it for general CCFA expenses. He said the chapter was under financial pressure and needed the surplus from the camp in order to meet its budget.

I went nuclear on him, which is not something I have done many times in my life. I was appalled. Not only was this a slimy move, but I also felt it was immoral. People made donations to Camp Oasis specifically to send a kid to camp—not to cover local chapter expenses. More than this, now that we had a good thing going and were generating surplus funding, the executive director wanted to take over the camp altogether.

I made a simple and impassioned speech to the members of the board, explaining that if this weasel got his way, I would resign from the board and devote all my time and money to running a camp that wasn't associated with the CCFA. It took a few weeks of back and forth politicking to eventually get others—who had been instrumental in getting the camp to its point of success—to convince the weasel to back down, let the camp be run as it had been, and allow the $20K surplus be used to fund the camp the next summer.

This deal was a little different from my other examples. The deal was to *not do the deal*—to stop the CCFA from using camp-directed funds for other uses. In this scenario, it would be fair to say that I was the rogue, but for very good reasons. Having the wisdom to know when to exercise this approach can be very powerful.

Postscript: Camp Oasis eventually moved to the Painted Turtle facility (part of Paul Newman's hole-in-the-wall gang of facilities) in Lake Hughes, California. It's a state of the art operation with a medical center on campus. The camp continues to this day. It has become so popular that it has added a second week each summer. A total of 220 kids from the LA area attend the camp each year.

KEY POINT IN THIS DEAL:

- When working on a nonprofit and doing so for altruistic reasons, DO NOT put up with bullshit from others who are simply looking to better their own positions and/or advance their own agendas.

MARK SUSTER
TIME IS THE ENEMY OF ALL DEALS

I first met Mark Suster back in 2007, when we were both members of a venture capital association in LA. He and I met about once a month in the early mornings on the west side of the city. At the time, Mark was very new to town and had just joined a VC firm called General Retail Partners (GRP).

Fast-forward a decade, and Mark is one of the most well known voices in venture capital. His blog "Both Sides of the Table" is widely read—not only by those looking to raise money but also by other VCs. The name is due to his experience as a two-time entrepreneur who has successfully sold both of his startups.

Since 2007, Mark has become the face of GRP, a firm he rebranded to Upfront Ventures in 2012 with the help of the partners. I am fortunate to count Mark as a friend. He is an investor and a very strong supporter of my current startup, HelloTech, for which he also acts as a board of directors observer.

In my conversations with Mark, he refers to himself as a "dot-com era baby," much the way our grandparents referred to themselves as "depression era babies." Mark's label means that he lived through the dot-com boom and its rather spectacular bust. It also means that much of his investing is informed by that history. Mark knows that boom times do not last and that when they bust, they seem to bust overnight. He has the heart and spirit of a startup CEO and the checkbook and wisdom of a venture capitalist.

Mark's first startup, Build Online, was a B2B commerce site based in Europe. They did their initial $2M seed financing in 1999 with some Irish investors who had a small fund. It became a super-hot company in January 2000. It seemed an overnight sensation. Everyone was trying to fund them. Not only the big VCs but also the larger investment banks. B2B commerce had become a very popular investment category, and the fame of Mark's company catapulted it to the *Financial Times*. He remembers the craziness of the boom period, when people were hunting down his home number to call to discuss investing in his company.

Mark realized back then, even before his first experience with a dot-com bust, that if he could get a strong balance sheet and de-risk his business, he needed to close the funding and put the money in the bank. Mark went with investors he felt would assist him most in growing his business (one of them was GRP, the firm he later joined), even though firms like Deutsche Telecom were offering him $1M under the table to win the investment.

Mark's instinct proved correct: GRP was very detailed-oriented, helping him review everything about the company more than once. He saw this as a value add because through that process, he refined his thinking to better position his company for success. The term sheet goal was to raise a $16.5M round led by GRP with an $8M check. The rest of the terms would be filled out with a syndicate (a common method by which early rounds are raised).

The syndicate was the easy part. In fact, Build Online was inundated by investors, all of whom desperately wanted in on the round. Morgan Stanley heard about the financing and flew a team to London to try to win the deal. Goldman Sachs said they would take his company public in just 18 months (knowing most companies didn't IPO for between seven and ten years). The company hadn't generated any revenue yet, so Goldman's proposal was an audacious, even ridiculous, one, but it was a sign of the times. Mark pulled the syndicate together quickly and closed the funding during the last week of February 2000. The markets crashed the following week.

Mark looks back on that deal and realizes just how lucky he was with the timing. There was no way anyone could have known the markets would crash the very next week. ALL funding stopped dead in its tracks.

With this reality deeply entrenched in his memory, Mark takes care to remind young entrepreneurs that there are always cycles in the market. He says, "When you have a decent deal on the table, close it ASAP." He warns against over-optimizing every dollar, which is a good way to find yourself out on the street with no funding at all. As Mark simply but eloquently put it, "Time is the enemy of all deals."

After closing the $16.5M round (in spite of the market collapse), Build Online was off to the races. They began producing as quickly as they could and built four distinct products in five different countries all at the same time. Mark now says of this, "It was just too much complexity all at once."

Morgan Stanley, which lost out on the investment, went ahead and funded a competitor with $60M, so Mark felt Build Online needed to work post-haste to stay ahead. He learned the lesson that any party who is not able to invest in your company is likely to fund a competitor, so be "very mindful in the funding negotiations."

Build Online was trying to stay ahead with product output, so they attempted to raise additional funds to remain on par with their competitor. While they had numerous promising conversations, investors had been spooked by the markets and kept backing out.

Eventually, Mark got JP Morgan and Goldman Sachs to agree to massive funding near a $100M valuation. At the time, Mark received some surprising advice from Yves Sisteron from GRP, who was on Build Company's board of directors. Yves said, "You're not worth that much money. If you take it, you will regret it. Cut your staff way back, cut your current product/country matrix way back, and raise a much lower amount. Focus on becoming a sustainable company (i.e., profitable)."

Mark took this advice. He made cuts according to advice offered up by a website called "Fucked Company." Popular at that time, the site featured companies that had had layoffs or been involved in business deals that had gone south. Mark was concerned that laying off a few people at a time would wreak havoc on the company, and everyone would worry whether their job was secure. So, in what Mark described as the worst day of his professional life, he went from 129 full-time employees all the way down to 38. (Side note: Anyone who has to do a Reduction in Force (RIF) would do well to follow Mark's example, and do it quickly.) Much to Mark's surprise, the company was able to get more done with that group of 38 than they had with 129.

Even with the cuts, Build Online quickly burned through their cash. A few months later, Mark found himself with only three weeks' worth. He assembled his team and explained the situation. He even went so far as to detail the bankruptcy process, should they head down that path. Just as the company was knocking on death's door, Mark received a call from GRP, who agreed to put in another $5M. Miraculously, Build Online also found another investor who agreed to put in $5M. It was April 2001, and the market was still dead, so the fact that they had been able to pull off the financing blew away Mark and his team.

Mark's decision to select GRP in the first place was affirmed. They proved they were truly a long-term partner. Mark was once again well funded, but this time with a much leaner operation. The lean mentality stuck with him all the way through the sale of his second startup to SalesForce. During the process of working on that deal, Mark constantly looked for ways to speed up the process, even by a few days or a week. He was worried the markets would change overnight, and the deal would be left on the table.

KEY POINTS IN THIS DEAL:

- You never know when the markets will fail. And when they do, investing can close overnight. If you have a good deal on the table with people you want to work with, close the deal and take the money off the table.

- When pitching your company to potential investors, realize you are educating them on an industry. If you excite them enough but don't take their money, they are likely to fund a competitor.

- Just because you raised a large financing round doesn't mean you should spend the money.

CHAPTER 9
FIGHTING AGAINST A MUCH LARGER INDUSTRY

SEAN RAD

ALIGN LONG-TERM VISION, THEN SWIPE RIGHT

I first met Sean in 2007 when he was working on his first startup, Orgoo. I was intrigued by the promise of his company, a web mail service that organized different mail accounts, contacts, and instant message friends all into one page. I saw a spark in Sean but did not foresee it was a characteristic of a rising star in the technology industry.

Now at the plump old age of 32, Sean is on his third startup: the hugely successful cultural phenomenon, Tinder. For those of you who have had your head buried in the sand or, like me, are old and married, Tinder is a dating site that introduced the concept of rapid-fire "swiping" (right to "like," left to "pass") photos of people to potentially meet, date, or hook up with. If two people swipe right on each other's photos, they are connected via the Tinder app and left to their own devices to meet. Users are connected only if they both swipe right, which means they get only positive feedback and connections. Swiping is a user experience paradigm that is now used across industries on hundreds of applications.

Sean hit a homerun with Tinder; one could even say a grand slam. It has become the primary app Millennials use to connect with each other, outdoing companies that have been in the matchmaking business for years, including eHarmony and Match.com. Currently, Tinder boasts 20B (that's billion with a "b") matches made, and they love to profile matches that have led to marriages and long-term relationships.

The app racks up 1.4B swipes/day, with 26M matches in over 196 countries. In November 2015, Tinder held its IPO and merged into the IAC conglomerate, which also owns Match.com, OK Cupid, and Expedia, among others. In March 2016, the market value for Tinder was a whopping $2.7B.

In mid-2015, I sat down with Sean at the worldwide head-quarters of Tinder, right in the middle of the famed Sunset Strip. We discussed the arc of his career, what lead him to Tinder, and his philosophy on deal making. He gave me some examples of when he believed he'd done the right thing, and one important lesson he learned when he did the wrong thing.

Sean's primary perspective on deal making, and on M&A trans-actions in particular, is to have a very frank and honest conversa-tion with the other party involved about their one-year and five-year objectives. Sean feels that if the parties can align on both of these objectives, there may be a foundation for a good deal. However, if the parties cannot align on these objectives, they do not have the makings of a good deal.

Even without an M&A conversation looming, Sean believes in constantly assessing his own company's one-year and five-year objectives. Because the technology industry moves so fast, competition comes and goes so quickly, and things can change literally overnight, Sean explained that he's diligent about ensuring his objectives remain relevant and realistic. He shared with me that while he had an idea of Tinder's five-year objectives early on in its life, it took a few years of actually growing the company for him to become very clear on them.

As Sean explained, when you are armed with a five-year perspective, you can scan the horizon for potential partners (companies you might merge with) and begin to make buy-versus-build decisions. First, does the other company's five-year objective align with yours? Second, will the companies' timetables be accelerated by putting them together? Third, will you be able to retain the top talent at the other company to end up with an additive and more powerful senior management team? Remember: If you proceed, you will need to give each of the teams joining forces control and accountability in order to make a real difference and provide the value, insight, and benefits you anticipated from the merger in the first place.

When Sean began negotiating the operational and financial relationship between Tinder and IAC, traction kicked in when the companies discussed each other's goals and motivations. From that point forward, the deal process went smoothly, and each party showed respect for the other's goals. When you understand what each party is trying to get out of the potential deal, you know whether to swipe right or left.

In spite of all of Tinder's success, Sean's best and most instructive story for *The Soul of a Deal* had to do with his second startup, Ad.ly. Sean founded Ad.ly in 2009 and served as its founder and president until early 2012. Ad.ly was ahead of its time with its mission of becoming celebrities' trusted platform for publishing posts on social media and anywhere else online. In sharing this anecdote, Sean was transparent about his mistakes. I found this very mature and refreshing. And, dear reader, I hope this story helps you.

Early on in Ad.ly's existence, Sean found himself in meetings with executives at the William Morris Agency, one of the top talent agencies in the world. A partnership between the two companies seemed like a natural fit. Ad.ly had developed technology that allowed celebrities to embrace and become part of the fast-growing social media world. William Morris represented top actors and musicians from around the globe who were all trying to understand how to use social media to expand their personal brands.

Sean admits that Ad.ly entered negotiations with William Morris with a bit too much ego in the game. They thought they could circumvent the talent agencies altogether and develop direct relationships with celebrities. There were a couple of things wrong with that assumption.

First, it didn't take into account Sean's key tenet, which he now regards as of the utmost importance: determine whether the one-year and five-year objectives of the two companies align. Second, Ad.ly had underestimated how hard it would be to unseat a talent agency, particularly a staple of the entertainment industry for 100 years.

In their overconfidence, Ad.ly expected far too much of an investment from William Morris. Because Ad.ly had overlooked the misaligned objectives of the two companies and expected too high of a price, they and William Morris parted ways. The deal was never consummated.

In hindsight, Sean feels that had Ad.ly's deal with William Morris moved forward, the partners would have been first to the market with Ad.ly's social media tools and become the market leaders. They may have even had a monopoly on social media tools for celebrities.

Instead, through the negotiation process, Ad.ly educated William Morris on the category. And when the deal fell apart, William Morris quickly created a competitive company called The Audience. In Sean's assessment, neither The Audience nor Ad.ly ever achieved the success individually that they would have achieved together. In effect, the industry became fragmented when Ad.ly, The Audience, and other competitors raced into the market.

The important lesson Sean learned through this process was that letting ego drive the ship gives you a false sense of your startup's ability. Ad.ly thought they could circumvent companies that had a huge presence in a long established industry. Instead, they ended up walking away from what could have been a transformative deal. In retrospect, Sean can see that he should have had more respect and appreciation for how challenging it is to change a long-standing industry. Now, he explained, he recognizes that understanding the way William Morris and other entrenched Hollywood players make deals would have helped Ad.ly at the negotiating table.

A couple of important things to note: The William Morris deal didn't kill Ad.ly by any means. The company is still in business and thriving today. However, not doing the deal decreased its potential, which added more risk. Not doing the deal also gave rise to a competitor, which left the industry fragmented.

In the end, Sean's experiences with Orgoo and Ad.ly showed him that the future was ALL ABOUT mobile, and this led to Tinder, so let's not feel sorry for Sean. He's doing just fine.

KEY POINTS IN THIS DEAL:

- When taking investment or negotiating an M&A deal, have a meaningful conversation early on about each organization's one-year and five-year goals to make sure these are aligned.

- Don't underestimate how challenging it can be for your startup to break into an entrenched industry.

DON'T TAKE ON
TWO 800-POUND GORILLAS

The late 1990s were a heyday for venture investing, especially in technology companies whose valuations bloated into the billions of dollars. When I became more active in angel investing, I was not investing alone. I was backed by two very well known, wealthy, and sophisticated investors: Michael Ovitz and Ron Burkle.

As the founder of Creative Artists Agency (CAA), Michael was essentially the "King of Hollywood." Ron was not as well known, I believe by choice, but he became a multi-billionaire by investing in, purchasing, and selling grocery store chains. Needless to say, working for them was quite fascinating. It gave me an opportunity to go from investing my own money (between $25K and $200K at a time) to investing significantly more ($4M to $80M), which led to much better and bigger deal flow.

One of the first companies we invested in was called Scour. Scour was far ahead of its time, and I recognized that. In short, it was a "broadband search engine." You must be thinking: What does that even mean? In 1999, it was a big deal to have a broadband Internet connection. (Read: high speed, like a 56K modem. Look that up on Wikipedia if you don't know what it is ;-).)

The exciting part about having a broadband Internet connection was that it allowed people to search for and find music, audio, and eventually video files. Scour excelled at this. At first, it focused on audio files, specifically MP3 files. It would "scour" the entire Internet, build an index of all the audio files on the web, and return the search results, giving users access to the content.

When I met the Scour founders, they were all computer science undergraduate students at UCLA, where I had received my degree some 15 years earlier. The core team was made up of three guys who were literally working out of their dorm rooms. We were able to cut a deal in which Michael, Ron, and I would purchase 50% of the company for $4M. This put an implied valuation on the company of $8M. However, the relationship got off to a very rocky start, and my co-investors and I should have taken that as a sign.

First, it's important to understand that the first step in most investment deals is an LOI (Letter of Intent). While an LOI is not binding (meaning neither party is legally committed to closing the deal), it almost always contains provisions designed to dissuade the company that is receiving the investment from having similar investment-oriented conversations with anyone else. In addition, the length of time specified in the LOI is often the amount of time the parties predict it will take to get the deal done. In many cases—some would say *most*—if the parties are moving forward in good faith and making progress toward closing the deal, and yet the deal does not close within the timeframe specified in the LOI, it's common that the parties will agree to extend the LOI.

In the case of the Scour deal, we had a non-binding, 30-day LOI, and we were moving as fast as we could to get the deal closed. As is often the case with deals of all types, ours with Scour did not close within 30 days, and my co-investors and I wanted to extend the LOI. Given that we had already invested time and money in the process and were acting in good faith to get the deal done, we expected Scour to agree to the extension. Unfortunately, however, the Scour team had no experience with LOIs or the common practice of extending them, and when the deal didn't close within 30 days, they felt it might not close at all. They became nervous and started talking to other parties about investing in Scour.

Needless to say, we were very unhappy about this. From our perspective, we were moving forward in good faith and expected Scour to understand this and sign an extension to the LOI. However, from Scour's perspective, our agreement with them was neither formal nor definitive. They worried our deal might not get done, and they wanted to take some time to decide if they wanted to proceed with us. The process even devolved into threats of legal action.

Years later and with the benefit of hindsight, I can see this should have been a HUGE red flag, and that I should have simply moved on and not been aggressive about closing the deal. That we had this level of disconnect and distrust so early in the process of what was likely to be a long and exhausting relationship should have been a message to both of our sides, especially (to be fair) to mine, which was made up of experienced and sophisticated investors. I can say now that we should have cut bait, cut our losses, and gone our separate ways. We would have been much better off. Scour might have been better off too. But we were seduced by the broadband space they were in and the opportunity they presented, so my team and I convinced ourselves to move forward. We worked through the disagreement with Scour and closed the deal.

To put the valuation at which we invested in Scour into perspective, the company had NO revenue. No money was being made on the searches, and the projected costs associated with running servers 24/7 and building the index of broadband content from all over the web were high.

The Scour founders, remember, were just college kids. They came to my Halloween party and got totally wasted and embarrassed themselves. We had serious meetings at my office over breakfast cereal. For the most part, they took my guidance and learned from me while Scour's search engine—in terms of the number of people using it to search for broadband content—got bigger and bigger every month.

It was the heyday of the Internet 1.0. Traffic and eyeballs were all anyone cared about. It wasn't even necessary to have a revenue-based business model early in a company's evolution. We did have a plan, however, given that we knew legitimate music services would be coming online to compete with services such as Scour and Napster, which was gaining traction then. We intended to sell ads to those legitimate services and take a revenue share for funneling people who searched for Elton John (or insert your favorite artist here) to a store where they could legally buy the content.

Less than a year into our investment in Scour, I received an inbound inquiry about the company from Rob Glaser, who was the Founder and Chairman/CEO of RealNetworks. Rob and I had gotten to know each other when I was president of Disney Online; Disney and ABC were some of RealNetworks' first big customers.

Rob and I had numerous conversations about the vision for Scour and how it fit quite well with the vision for RealNetworks. Once our conversations had progressed to the point where I believed Real was likely to make an offer to buy Scour, I began sharing the details of these conversations with Michael, Ron, and the Scour kids. After several discussions, we agreed we were open to selling the company if the price was right. We also agreed I would lead the negotiations, given my relationship with Rob. My understanding was that it would be "dope" if we could get $40M or $50M for the company. Little did I know I was wrong.

Armed with all the details, I began a negotiation with RealNetworks, specifically with Rob. We went back and forth many times, but within just a few weeks, we had settled on a number: $55M (in spite of the fact that Scour still had $0 in revenue). I remember the offer came in on the confidential fax machine in my office. I thought the number was a huge win, especially as first a written offer. Traditionally, you never accept the first formal written offer you receive; in most cases, there's room to negotiate the amount and terms.

I wanted to make sure the offer was real (pun intended) before involving the Scour team because I did not want to distract them. While my intentions were good, holding this information back ended up causing a problem. I was not prepared for was just how much residue and lack of trust existed between the Scour team and us. (See the beginning of this chapter where I say we should have never done the deal).

Given the mistrust the LOI issue had created, the Scour team falsely assumed I was negotiating behind their backs and trying to cut them a shitty deal. (Their presumption was misguided, as I could not force a deal on them with our 50/50 ownership structure.) The residue from the LOI misunderstanding made them suspicious that I did not have their best interests at heart.

Formal offer in hand, I proudly shared it with the Scour team. The deal would increase the company's value from $8M to $55M (a factor of 700%) in less than a year. To be fair, it was structured in a way that the cash investors (Michael and Ron) would have an immediate cash payout. The Scour team would get their payout in cash and stock and would need to remain employees of RealNet-works for quite some time.

This type of arrangement was (and still is) fairly common in acquisitions of very early-stage companies because the founding teams of these companies tend to be their most valuable asset. None-theless, the contrast between the way the cash investors would be paid and the way the Scour team would be paid only heightened Scour's mistrust—especially because they were not experienced in this type of acquisition.

The next morning, during my drive to the office, I received a phone call. Right away, I knew it was bad news. The Scour team had gathered together the night before and decided that if they could get $55M from RealNetworks, they might be able to get much more ($100M or more) from either RealNetworks or another bidder. I know as well as anyone that most deals have room for negotiation, but I had worked for some time with Rob to get to the $55M offer. It had not simply come through on the first day. I also knew Real's appetite for a startup that was burning cash with no revenue would not double to $100M.

I asked the Scour team what their plan was, and they told me they were going to leak the offer from RealNetworks to the press. Specifically, they were going to send the information to an online news agency called CNET to see whether this would surface other bidders and/or get Real to increase their offer. I recall they believed Microsoft was a potential bidder.

You must remember, this was the initial Wild West of the Internet. Companies were being purchased for hundreds of millions of dollars. I don't think the Scour team appreciated my skill or ability in negotiating deals. They had no idea how much back and forth it took to get that $55M offer, not to mention the value of my close professional relationship with Rob. They didn't trust that I had their best interests at heart, and they naively thought they could do better.

I pleaded with them not to move forward with the leak. We had a bona fide written offer, which had been negotiated in good faith over the course of a few weeks. I understood Rob well and knew he would unquestionably back out if Scour took this tack. I warned Scour that the $55M offer could be negotiated, but not in the public court of press leaks. To leak the offer could easily turn it into nothing, I told them, and we would be back to the drawing board, trying to figure out how to generate revenue from their nascent business.

My next call was to Rob. I felt I owed him a heads up. He deserved to know that the Scour team was not enthusiastic about the deal and that I needed some time with them to work things through. He agreed to this.

By the time I had made it to the office, Scour had already leaked the story. To add insult to injury, they had leaked it from my office! I couldn't believe it. Here were these kids who had never done a business deal of any size in their lives, going over my head and upending the negotiations. In fact, the story they leaked was that RealNetworks had offered them $100M.[9] When I saw the story, I knew the RealNetworks deal was dead.

Not surprisingly, Rob called me within the next hour. He was infuriated. He asked how the press leak got out. I told him I wasn't sure, but I was working on it. Then he asked outright if the Scour team was behind it, and I couldn't lie. (Straight-up lies come at too

---

9   https://www.cnet.com/news/real-bids-close-to-100-million-for-scour-net/

high of a cost: the sacrifice of your long-term reputation.) Predictably, Rob told me the deal was off. He said he didn't want to do business with people that conducted a negotiation in this fashion, and he sent a fax rescinding the offer.

That afternoon, I met with the Scour kids and asked what they wanted to do. They still wanted to see if we could get some other party to make an offer for $100M or more. I made a few calls, but there were no bites. Still, they tried to show good face and mentioned some ideas for growing the business that would make it worth "well more than $55M."

A few days later, the dust had settled, and I called Rob to ask if we could resurrect the offer. He stayed true to his word. He said the Scour team were simply not the kind of people he wanted to do business with. He also told me Scour had already reached out to him, post press leak, to try and negotiate the price. He told them he no longer had any interest.

During the next few weeks, I met with the Scour team, and they outlined their plans to develop and release a new product called Scour Exchange. We were in the heyday of Napster and all the lawsuits against them by music labels who charged the company was supporting illegal music-file sharing and distribution. The Scour Exchange product, as it was explained to me, was exactly the same as Napster. However, it could share/distribute any type of file over a peer-to-peer file sharing network, which meant people could share movies and TV shows in addition to music. I was incredulous. They planned not only to go down the same path of a company that was being sued for billions of dollars, but also to extend that path to the TV and movie industries.

I explained what Scour's fate would be if they proceeded (massive lawsuits), but the team felt they had some ways around the law, and they wanted to move forward ASAP with the release of Scour Exchange. The future was very clear to me: Scour would be sued by both the RIAA and the MPAA (two very powerful and well funded lobbying groups representing the music industry and the movie industry).

Given the importance of my reputation to my business dealings in addition to the fact that I was involved in several startup media companies, had until recently been president of Disney Online, and did not want to be dragged into a protracted lawsuit, I felt I had no choice but to immediately resign from Scour's board of directors. I made public statements to that effect, making it clear that I didn't want anyone in the media industry (a relatively small world in LA) to think that I was in any way involved with Scour Exchange.[10]

Unfortunately for all the investors, the Scour team did go on to release Scour Exchange exactly as they'd described. In short order, Scour was sued by both the RIAA and the MPAA for hundreds of billions of dollars. (Yes, billions with a B). Needless to say, the investment community was immediately turned off from the company. Scour filed for bankruptcy protection, and all its assets were sold at auction to the highest bidder. The Scour kids received no money.

There are a few important aspects of this deal that turned it sour. First and most importantly, the relationship between the investors and the company started off with a lack of trust. Above all else, this was the root of the entire deal going south. Second was the Scour kids' inexperience. This was what drove their overconfidence and

---

10 http://variety.com/2000/digital/news/scour-goes-sour-1117787803/

their ill-fated decision to attempt to fetch a $100M acquisition offer by leaking the RealNetworks deal to the press.

Postscript: In full disclosure, most of the Scour kids have gone on to be very successful entrepreneurs. They were indeed a talented bunch, and with any luck, they learned from the RealNetworks experience. One of the founders was Travis Kalanick. A young man attracted to disrupting authority, he is now known around the world as the (former) CEO and co-founder of Uber. Two decades after co-founding Scour, Travis was willing to use the same negotiation tactics he had with RealNetworks with the transportation industry—only this time, they paid off immeasurably. He created a company with a market cap north of $60B and has a personal net worth of more than $5B. So while Scour may have been the wrong company at the wrong time, Uber certainly allowed Travis to hit his stride.

KEY POINTS IN THIS DEAL:

- If you lose trust at the beginning of a business partnership, cease moving forward ASAP. Wish each other well and walk the other way. Mistrust festers and gets in the way of collaboration. It prevents both sides from working together toward a mutually beneficial outcome.

- In the height of a business negotiation, you cannot be directly untruthful to the other parties engaged in the deal.

- If you are working with young founders and you are negotiating a deal on their behalf, make sure they know and understand the process. Keep them apprised along the way, so they understand what it takes to get to a formal written offer. Throughout the process, show you are considering everyone's interests.

- It does not work to publicize a hard-earned offer in the hopes it will lead to a much higher offer. More likely than not, the original offer will be pulled, and you will end up with nothing.

- Be careful breaking into a multi billion-dollar industry that is well organized and well funded. For example, you don't want to piss off lobbying groups like the RIAA or MPAA—they'll combat anything that's a threat to their business. However, if you find a niche that is not well organized or funded, disruption, innovation, and transformation can really pay off.

- If you do find an industry that is ripe for disruption, as Travis finally did in transportation, and that industry does not have a well funded lobbying group, then you can be disruptive with much less risk of being shut down.

LARRY LESSIG
THAT SECOND $5M WAS JUST TOO HARD

I feel fortunate to call Larry Lessig a friend. He's a genius when it comes to the evolving landscape of the Internet and the various legal questions and challenges it raises. After writing several successful books and teaching at Stanford for years, Larry was hired away in 2009 by Harvard to serve as the Roy L. Furman Professor of Law.

During the last decade, Larry's focus has shifted from the impact of the Internet to the issue of campaign finance reform. He's shown a light on how less than 1% of the U.S. population's wealth effectively controls which political figures get elected via their Super Pac fundraising.

Larry's passion for advocacy is so strong that a few years back he started an organization called MAYDAY America, whose aim is straightforward:

"Our democracy has been hijacked by a handful of super wealthy corporations and families. The framers of our Constitution envisioned a democracy that was representative of all citizens, not the wealthiest 1%. It now costs millions of dollars to get and stay elected for any meaningful political role. This means our representatives are indebted to large donors to fund their elections and as a result are inappropriately influenced."

As shared on the MAYDAY America website, Larry outlines a solution: "Pass model legislation to create constitutional, small-donor elections and dismantle the concentrated power in our government." Central to this are reforms that fix gerrymandering, impose term limits, and protect voting rights. Making these reforms a reality requires electing candidates who "believe in empowering the many, not the few."[11] As Larry has explained, it is necessary to elect a critical mass of state and local champions who support fundamental reform from the ground up and, as a result, force Congress to act or get out of the way.

Larry believed that to make this happen, he had to raise the Super Pac to end all Super Pacs—one that would support and help get elected politicians who would not be indebted to the wealthiest 1% (who now support most candidates for political office). But how could he do a deal to make such a transformational act occur?

Larry decided to launch the fundraising for MAYDAY America via a Ted Talk, several of which he's been called upon to deliver. Larry has an amazing mastery of deep intellectual topics and a keen ability to share and educate people on them in an engaging and captivating manner. Challenging the political power of the nation's wealthiest 1% was no small task, and Larry was unlikely to achieve this objective in a short timeframe. Adding to this, most experts couldn't see how MAYDAY America would result in real change. Nevertheless, Larry remained undaunted and committed to experimenting in order to figure out how to make MAYDAY America work.

In his now infamous Ted Talk, Larry announced what he hoped to do with MAYDAY America. He mapped out a strategy that bounced between small donors and big donors. He planned to start with small donors to get to an initial contribution of $1M in 30 days, at which point he would shift focus to bigger donors to get the first

---

11 Source: MAYDAY.US, https://mayday.us/the-plan/.

$1M matched within the next 30. Following that, he would work through small donors to raise $5M within 30 days and then use that momentum to go back to bigger donors to match that $5M within the next 30. Assuming he could accomplish these goals, MAYDAY America would be funded with $12M, which he felt was enough to support some independent candidates (those not backed by the wealthiest 1% or indebted to anyone) and get a handful elected to important offices. Larry thought this would be a great start of what he expected would be a ten-year effort.

However, as Larry learned, he was completely wrong about what he assumed would be hard and what would be easy about fundraising. Going into the process, Larry believed that raising money from the small donors would prove a time-consuming and difficult task. He also believed that once he had those initial commitments, it would be quicker and more straightforward to raise the matching funds from wealthier donors who were supportive of his goals and campaign finance reform. He actually found the opposite to be true.

Much to his surprise, Larry reached the first goal of raising $1M in just 13 days. Then he turned to some bigger donors he was connected with. In the end, it proved much harder and more time-consuming to match the $1M than it had been to raise it in the first place. Ultimately, however, Larry was successful.

In the next phase, Larry had a deadline of July 4th to raise $5M from small donors. There were many days (most of them, in fact) when Larry was concerned MAYDAY America would not achieve its goal. However, much to his surprise and pleasure, the organization managed to raise the $5M within the desired timeframe. Then he turned his attention once again to securing the matching $5M from larger donors. Larry thought this process would be a relatively smooth one. But it turned into what he referred to as a "nightmare experience."

In retrospect, Larry said, it makes sense that raising the matching $5M was more difficult than he'd thought it would be. For one thing, he learned that very wealthy people often have short attention spans. What is important to them one month may not be as important to them the next. For another, he found himself the victim of the exact problem he was trying to solve: He was in a position where he was too dependent on a group of wealthy people for funds.

Larry says he would do many things differently if he could fundraise all over again. One is that he would put a cutoff date on the timeframe for matching the $5M. This would limit the time he spent on fundraising. During the summer of 2016, he continued to chase down big investors to meet the $5M goal, and the process simply went on for far too long.

Although MAYDAY America's fundraising efforts were successful overall (Larry and his team raised $11M out of the $12M goal), as the organization sought money from some of its wealthy donors, they found they had to compromise on some of their original goals. In other words, they fell victim to the exact influence Larry was trying to minimize. A case in point: Larry developed the strategy for determining which elections MAYDAY America would get involved with and which candidates they would support. However, once they'd received money from billionaires, MAYDAY America had to deal with inbound, unsolicited, and sometimes unhelpful suggestions regarding which political races the organizations should focus on. Larry felt somewhat beholden to the billionaires, and as a result, the organization did get involved in some of the suggested races, effectively undermining the exact process they were trying to fix.

As Larry and I discussed this process, he reflected that, in hindsight, he realizes he should have foregone the match. He should have focused on the initial $1M to get a lot of attention and then pursued smaller donors for the next $5M. With this $6M in hand, Larry could have gone to work effecting the change he sought, spending more time on the organization's efforts and less time soliciting or managing the donors from the wealthiest 1%.

As he thought it through, Larry came full circle on some of his initial thoughts. He had assumed the involvement of the super wealthy would be essential. Looking back, however, he believes the process would have been far more streamlined and successful without them.

Another interesting negotiation took place during this time (a deal within the deal, if you will) between Larry and Stephen Colbert. The comedian had announced he was going to raise a Super Pac to affect political races, and when Larry learned of Colbert's intentions, he sat down with the talk show host and suggested they work together. To Larry, it seemed like a good partnership: Larry understood the law and its true implications better than Colbert, and Colbert had a bigger platform for raising funds via his late night show.

Unfortunately, Colbert was not interested in combining the two initiatives. Nevertheless, Larry requested that Colbert host him on his show so that Larry could promote his efforts and reach an important demographic. For months, Colbert sort of teased Larry, letting him believe he was open to having Larry as a guest. In the end, Colbert didn't deliver, which caused Larry to question the comedian's motives. In the meantime, however, Larry carried on, demonstrating a gallant effort through November 2016, when MAYDAY America did not win as many seats in the election as they had hoped.

KEY POINTS IN THIS DEAL:

- When trying to transform a business sector, be careful not to become part of the exact process you are trying to fix.

- Never underestimate how difficult it is to close deals with billionaires.

MARC GEIGER

BE THE LITTLE DOG THAT SNARLS
BACK AT THE BIGGER DOG

I first met Marc Geiger back in the late 1990s, when I was working for Michael Ovitz and Ron Burkle. My primary job was running a company we'd started called CheckOut.com, which leveraged Ron's massive grocery empire to deliver CDs and DVDs to local grocery stores for free. But I also acted as the lead investor in technology companies on behalf of Michael and Ron.

During this time, I led the acquisition of a company called Alliance Entertainment Corporation. Alliance was a major provider of retail services to Marc's company ARTISTdirect, a company he had founded in 1994. Once I'd led the acquisition of Alliance, I ended up working closely with Marc. (Alliance provided all of the retail management and shipping of artist-related merchandise sold by ARTISTdirect.) During this time, Marc and I became friends, and we remain so today.

As a key partner to ARTISTdirect, Alliance was invested in helping the company reach its potential. And to be sure, Marc was well ahead of his time. His vision was that artists could establish direct relationships with their fan bases (thus the name ARTISTdirect) and over time, cut the label out and sell their music and merchandise directly to customers. ARTISTdirect was a leader in its field by virtue of the progress Marc had made in partnering with the labels and getting them to buy into his vision.

ARTISTdirect was founded in 1994, during the very early days of digital music, and by 2000, the company was in the process of raising its Series C round to prepare for its upcoming IPO. For Marc, the importance of the Series C round was to get ALL of the labels to invest. This way, he could be sure their interests were aligned with his and that he would not fall prey to their lawsuits. (In fact, leading up to the Series C, Sony Music was suing Marc, but he was able to turn them around.) In a deal that was unprecedented at the time, Marc was able to raise a Series C round totaling $85M that included participation from every major music label. Their involvement speaks to the respect the industry players had (and still have) for him.

At the time, there were two big portal companies: Yahoo and AOL. Conventional wisdom held that if you wanted to get meaningful traffic for your business, you needed a major partnership with at least one of them. As such, as part of the $85M in funding ARTISTdirect pulled in from the major labels, they agreed to two very deep and very expensive partnerships: one with Yahoo and one with Ticketmaster.

Both of the deals seemed pretty straightforward. They involved section buyouts whereby ARTISTdirect would effectively own and control the content and inventory in the music section. For Ticketmaster, it was a permanent category buyout of artist merchandise and goods. In effect, ARTISTdirect bought the e-commerce section attached to the ticket sale, for which they paid Ticketmaster $7M up front.

The Yahoo deal was much more substantial. ARTISTdirect took some of the $85M they had raised and spent $20M to buy Yahoo's entire music category. In exchange, in a deal structure that was popular in the late 90s (especially with what AOL called "round-tripping"), Yahoo took $2.5M of that $20M and invested it back into ARTISTdirect in exchange for equity. Round-tripping is not only bad business, but it could also be illegal, depending on how it's handled. This type of transaction sent the CEO of HomeStore.com to jail!

Nevertheless, Marc felt pretty good about these deals. He thought they would position ARTISTdirect as the leader for the music industry across the web. Marc was also banking on something that seemed fundamental to him in business: When you did a deal and held up your end of the agreement, the other party would make good on their end in turn. This presupposition turned out to bite him in the ass.

With the Ticketmaster and Yahoo deals signed, ARTISTdirect prepared to go public. They interviewed banks, ultimately choosing Morgan Stanley. Everything seemed to be going smoothly. Marc's years of hard work and deal making were about to pay off in the form of a successful IPO, when out of nowhere, Yahoo decided in a strategic move to make music a "focus category." This meant that even though they'd previously sold ARTISTdirect the music category, they were going to compete directly with the company. All of the links would no longer go to ARTISTdirect; instead, they would direct to Yahoo's own music pages.

At that point, Marc was faced with a massive decision. He had just paid Yahoo $17.5M (because $2.5M of the $20M came back in the form of investment), and the company had ignored the terms of their agreement with ARTISTdirect. When Marc confronted Yahoo, they simply said, "Sue us." He had to decide if he should sue Yahoo, which would indefinitely postpone and potentially derail the IPO, or swallow the bitter pill and move forward.

As Marc told me this story, he recalled thinking: "How do you deal with somebody who is clearly and blatantly in breach of contract? They take your money and then turn around and fuck you by lying about what you thought you'd all agreed to."

This was a tremendously stressful time for Marc as a first-time CEO of a soon-to-be-public company. After much discussion with his management team and bankers, Marc decided the lawsuit would be a distraction and potentially do more harm than good. Ultimately, Marc and his team chose not to go after the "800-pound gorilla that was Yahoo at that point in time." To them, it didn't make sense to interfere with the IPO and waste funds in the process.

Still, in retrospect, Marc questions the decision they made. He feels he was too influenced by the banks, who were unilaterally focused on the fees they would make by taking a company public. Today, he asks himself: "Why did I listen to the banks? Did I really have to jump through the hoops they set up for me?"

Marc and his team faced a series of choices at a critical point in ARTISTdirect's history, and ultimately, they took what seemed like the easy path: not to fight. Marc remembered, "At the time, I was accused of making the pussy choice to just get ripped off while I shook my fists and yelled, 'God damn you, Yahoo! You're a mean, fucked up company.' Then again, I have regret, which is why it sticks with me. I regret that I chose to be a pussy rather than being tenacious and protecting my rights and turf. I should have been that little dog that snarls back at the bigger dog and is fearless over what is right—not what might be right for the business."

KEY POINTS IN THIS DEAL:

- Making a business deal with another party—even a deal with very clear terms—does not guarantee the other party will deliver on their end.

- Don't be intimidated by bigger companies with more resources. If you have been wronged and have a strong legal case, retain good counsel and go after them.

CHAPTER 10
BEING YOUNG ENOUGH TO TAKE THE RISK

PENN JILLETTE

MOSTLY, WE JUST SAY "YES"... AND YOU COULD HAVE GOTTEN US FOR LESS

As most of you know, Penn Jillette is the vocal half of the world-famous entertainment pair Penn & Teller. I am fortunate enough to count him as a friend. I first met Penn in the late 90s through a mutual friend. He was intrigued by my career as a successful Internet dude, and I was intrigued simply by the fact that he was Penn Jillette.

Over the last 20 years, Penn and I have shared several meals together. I've seen his show many times and have had the pleasure of sitting down with him and discussing various topics. During our conversations, he typically eats his favorite dish of grilled salmon.

What has stood out for me the most—and what I want to make sure I share with all of you—is just how smart Penn is. IMHO (in my humble opinion), he is brilliant. He is deeply passionate about his work and truly cares about entertaining his fans. He is well versed on a surprising number of topics and can hold his own in an intellectual conversation about just about anything.

His gratitude to his fans is demonstrated after each show when he stays behind for as long as it takes to sign autographs for anyone who wants one. He refers to each of his fans as "Boss," which is his way of acknowledging that he works for them.

In January 2015, Penn and I sat down to discuss *The Soul of a Deal* after one of his shows in Vegas. He shared with me how he and Teller have approached deal making throughout their 30-year career.

Penn is very conscientious when it comes to making deals. He told me he won't do a deal unless he is willing to sign for the other side as well. This approach has served him very well in his career, as people have come to know him as a fair and trustworthy businessperson.

Penn's strategy for getting deals done: "Mostly, we just say 'yes.'" Penn attributes this to his upbringing in a working-class family, one that mirrors Teller's. Penn's father was a jail guard, and Teller's father was a commercial artist. When, early in their careers, the pair started making more money than their dads by focusing exclusively on the one thing they loved to do, they found it "breathtaking."

From the earliest days of their business, Penn and Teller were wary of trusting a third party to manage it, so they did everything themselves. They didn't just do the negotiating, they managed the whole deal—the finances and accounting, everything. Worried this practice might make them appear amateur-ish to potential clients, they invented a fictitious company, "Bugs and Rooney," and referred to it as their "management team." People didn't realize that Penn was "Bugs" and Teller was "Rooney." Penn would be on the phone negotiating and say things like, "I'll run it by Penn and Teller, but I don't know if they're going to go for it."

Through operating as Bugs and Rooney, Penn told me, they became experts at protecting themselves from contracts' downsides. They learned to put clauses in their agreements such as: "If there are fewer than 'X' people in the audience, Penn & Teller will not have to perform, but they will still receive their minimum payment for traveling and setting up for the show." The two didn't leave home for a show until they received all of the travel money up front, so they were never left holding the bag on overhead costs or expenses without enough cash to return home.

Penn and Teller also had very specific terms in their agreements, such as "No Chinese." While racist and politically incorrect, this reference dates back to the old Carnie days (sideshow circus acts), when immigrant Chinese workers were responsible for loading and unloading the circus trucks. In Penn & Teller's contracts, it meant they did not load or unload their own stuff.

Penn certainly has come a long way from when he started out as a young street performer. Now, he's half of an act that headlines five nights a week at The Rio Hotel in Las Vegas. He and Teller have a dedicated theater with their names on it.

Penn recalled an exchange he had with the woman from the Rio who was responsible for all of the entertainment at the hotel. Penn told me, "We were at a charity function just after signing the

Rio deal. She'd had a drink or two, and she said, 'You know, Penn, you could have gotten more money out of us,' to which I replied, 'And you could have gotten us for less money.'" To Penn, this was an optimal deal; both sides felt they had gotten the better end of the deal, and neither side felt taken advantage of.

Penn fondly remembered another moment from earlier in his career, when he was 30, and Teller was about 35. They had roughly $100K in savings between them, which seemed like a lot of money. They were both single at the time without families to support. Their parents were healthy, their earnings were strong, and most importantly, they had jobs doing the work they loved—work they would do for free, which is why they were so amenable to saying "yes" to most deals.

Penn recounted various deals he and Teller did not for the money, but for the promotion and exposure. One example he gave me was his stint on *Celebrity Apprentice*. Penn said he was really torn about doing one of "those silly Trump shows." While he was pleased that all of the proceeds from the challenges went to charities that the celebrities chose, he had an aversion to the "Trump" way of doing deals, which requires that there be a winner and a loser. "It goes against everything I believe in when trying to strike a mutually beneficial business deal for all parties involved," Penn said. "It all comes back to Teller's and my default behavior to say "yes" to almost anything, which stems back to when we were kids, fearing we would be stuck in the small town we grew up in—in my case, Greenfield [Massachusetts]. It still drives me today. I'm terrified that if I say 'no' to an opportunity, the 17-year-old boy in me is going to bitch slap me and say 'Fuck You, Penn Jillette.'"

Fast forward 20+ years, and Penn & Teller were able to get the marquis performance for the Rio Hotel in Vegas with a theater dedicated to their show (meaning they could rehearse the full show whenever they wanted, which was critical to their ability to explore new things and try them out). In this deal, the investors were the shareholders of the casino who they were far more focused on how much money they made on gambling than they were on any particular show.

Penn recalls, "We hardly see the man who is our boss now. Every year and a half, we bump into him, and he goes, 'Stop by the office and let me know how the show is going.' I tell him, 'We got about 40 minutes of new material,' and he goes, 'Oh, good.' He'll come to the show and bring his nephew in. Every three years, he'll get an autograph. I'm not even convinced that he's actually watched the show. It's very possible he left his relatives in there while he was out on the cell phone, making deals."

Although Penn and Teller work very well together professionally, the match was not an obvious one. Penn was still in high school when they met. Teller was a magician who made a living teaching English and Classics. Teller took a liking to Penn, and at the end of a long day of the teenager performing on the street, Teller would come by and take him out to dinner. The pair talked about crazy ideas for a show they could work on together. This was the genesis for all of the Penn & Teller bits we know today!

Penn was the duo's primary driver at the time. His street performing had begun to get recognized. When various venues called him to book a show, he said he'd do it only if he could bring his magician friend, Teller. Penn didn't ask the venues for additional money; he offered to pay Teller out of his own. (This is further proof that Penn stays true to what he believes in and values this more than the money he could make from any given gig.) As Penn continued to book gigs for himself and Teller, he pressed his friend into performing full-time. Teller, however, was reluctant to give up his teaching job.

As Penn shared with me, "I called up Teller in July, I guess. I said, 'I've got a real professional gig for you.' Teller was doing a show in, like, church basements and stuff. I said, 'I've got a real professional show for you, and you'll get paid to do shows in front of the public out in Minnesota.' 'When does it start?' Teller asked. 'It starts in the middle of August,' I replied. 'Oh! Great. When does it end?' Teller asked. 'Ends, uh, the fourth week of October,' I said. 'Oh, I'll be back teaching,' Teller said. 'The school year starts in September, so don't think I can do this with you, Penn.'"

Penn appealed to Teller's true passion, saying, "I just thought you were a magician, not a teacher, my mistake." And fifteen minutes later, the phone rang. It was Teller, who said, "I'm not going to quit teaching. I will not quit teaching. I'm not going to do that. I'm tenured, I like my job, and it's a good, steady job. I will not quit teaching. I will take a year of absence—a sabbatical. I can do that. I can talk to the principal. I will do these shows, and I will write shows with you, and I will work on it, and I have a little bit of savings and can do one year, and that's it." September has come and gone for several decades now, and Teller never mentions going back to teaching.

KEY POINTS IN THIS DEAL:

- Would you sign the other side's end of the deal? Use that question as a litmus test to see what you think it is fair.

- Sometimes, you need to appear larger than you are.

- Sometimes, the non-financial aspects of a deal/gig are equally as important as the money.

MELLODY HOBSON
SOMETIMES, NAIVETÉ IS YOUR BEST ASSET

I have been fortunate enough to know Mellody Hobson for about 20 years. Mellody is one of those people who gets so much done at such a high level of competence, integrity, and passion, that I honestly don't quite know how she does it.

In addition to being the president of the Chicago-based Ariel Investments, where she has worked since joining the firm as an intern before graduating college, Mellody is also the chairman of the board of DreamWorks SKG, serves on the board of Starbucks, is a regular contributor to CBS, and still manages to find time for her beautiful young daughter and her husband, George Lucas.

I had no idea where my interview with Mellody would take us, given that she has a hand in so many interesting endeavors and has accomplished so much for someone who is still quite young. When we sat down to discuss potential stories that would be instructive for *The Soul of a Deal*, Mellody quickly narrowed in on a deal she orchestrated early in her career at Ariel. It was a deal, she confided, that could have either made or broken her career with the firm. Given what I've told you about Mellody, you can already guess which way it went, but the details are fascinating.

Mellody joined Ariel in 1991. She jokes that she is the only person she knows who has ever had only one work phone number. She skipped the traditional MBA route, becoming so entrenched and successful at Ariel that her work there became her on-the-job MBA.

The deal Mellody shared with me shared with me took place in 1994. She shared this deal with me because consummating it required that she put her job on the line and because in retrospect, she realizes it was a deal that informed her entire career at Ariel.

In 1994, Ariel had a joint venture with a mutual fund partner called the Calvert Group. Based in Bethesda, Calvert had been around longer than Ariel. Calvert managed the marketing and distribution for the joint fund, and Ariel managed the assets.

As Mellody recalled, although she was just "the pipsqueak that worked at Ariel," she believed the company needed to separate from Calvert. She thought Ariel had the potential to build its own brand and reputation, and that doing this would be challenging so long as the company was captive in a joint fund. Mellody first went to Ariel founder, John Rogers. To her surprise and delight, John agreed with her. Together they went to Ariel's board of directors, and again, somewhat to her surprise, they also embraced the idea that Ariel should separate from Calvert.

This suggestion of Mellody's was a bold one because the companies' partnership had been working well; the funds represented quite a bit of money and had great returns. Plus, the companies had been partners since 1986, well before Mellody had come to work at Ariel. Yet, she felt the two brands stood for different things. Ariel represented patient, long-term value investing, while Calvert's focus put socially responsible investing front and center. While Ariel also believed (and still does) in socially responsible investing, this was a matter of emphasis for the firm rather than a guiding principle.

When I asked Mellody what gave her the courage to make such a bold suggestion when she was just a few years out of school and still early in her tenure at Ariel, she thought long and hard before answering. Then she came to the simple conclusion that it had been pure naiveté. "If I knew then what I know now," she said, "I probably would have never had the courage to do it."

Mellody's comment about naiveté in deals is a key point for *The Soul of a Deal*. Many people in their 20s and 30s are still in early enough stages of their careers to be willing to take BIG risks. Often, as people become more settled in their careers, particularly during their 40s and 50s, they develop less tolerance for risk. If you're more advanced in age and your career, when thinking about taking audacious steps, ask yourself what your younger 20-something self would do.

After getting agreement from Ariel's management team and board of directors, Mellody and John took the next step of going to the Calvert Group's management team and the Calvert-Ariel fund's board of directors and asking for a divorce. Mellody remembers the details of the trip to Bethesda almost to the tee. She recalls flying there with John and how, as the flight went on, he became more and more uncomfortable.

When they landed, John told Mellody he was quite anxious about the decision and that he needed to call his mentor and coach, Pete Carroll, to get advice. As Mellody recalled, John told her that as soon as Pete answered the phone, he knew from John's tone of voice that something was not right. Pete asked John, "What's bothering you? I can hear the discomfort in your voice and in your breathing," and John explained to Pete, "I'm doing something I've never done before. I'm asking someone for a divorce, and I am quite anxious about it."

Once John and Ariel presented the breakup proposal to the management team at Calvert, the team responded that they planned to go to the board of directors of the joint fund to get guidance on whether and how they should move forward. A few weeks later, John and Mellody returned to Calvert and made their presentation to the joint board. The two were very clear in what they were asking for: They wanted to terminate the partnership. The board listened, and as soon as the presentation was over, they said they were going to go into an executive session. For those of you not familiar with this term, "executive session" means the board meets without any of the full-time staff from the companies. The people on the board try to figure out the best overall decision for all of the shareholders of the company without being influenced or swayed by any of its active executives.

The Calvert/Ariel executive session went on for two hours, during which John and Mellody sat in the hall and waited. Eventually, the board called the two teams back in and told them, "Listen, here's the deal. You have one month to come to terms on what Ariel will pay to leave, and in that time, you can't talk to any of us." By setting it up this way, the board ensured that neither side could lobby board members directly. The management teams from each side needed to work to figure out what Ariel was willing to pay to get the desired separation.

The board also told John, Mellody, and the Calvert team that if they couldn't come to a mutually agreeable solution within one month, the board could choose to take the money from the joint fund and move it into a third-party fund. This would have been disastrous for both Ariel and Calvert. That's right: Now, Ariel not only had to negotiate with their counterparts, they also faced the threat of losing management of the joint fund if the two companies failed to come up with a mutually beneficial agreement.

This was a big blow to the Ariel team. All of a sudden, they realized it was all or nothing. There was no going back to the way things were. Either they came up with a deal, or they lost the fund altogether. John was a bit distraught over this situation. Mellody now speculates that he was thinking, "Oh my God, I let this new woman talk me into this, and now I could lose everything."

The next month was filled with nonstop work and sleepless nights as John, Mellody, and the rest of the Ariel team tried to come up with a deal that would work for both parties. Ultimately, Ariel agreed to pay $4M for the right to manage $400M of the fund's assets. At that point in Ariel's history, $4M was their life savings. It was every dime the company had in reserves. In advance of the deadline set by the Calvert-Ariel fund board, John and Mellody returned to Bethesda and presented their proposal, and the joint board accepted it. It was June, and the board told the Ariel and Calvert teams that they had until Labor Day to affect the separation.

A fresh start after the holiday was a good plan, and the two companies spent the summer breaking the funds apart. It was the first time either had done anything like it. At the end of the day, each mutual fund shareholder would be able to choose which fund they wanted their money to go with. That the companies had to go through this process illustrates that a deal sometimes has to go through several stages before it gets done. Just getting approval from the board to work on breaking up the funds seemed like a victory, yet as soon as that victory was over, the real work began.

The entire summer that Mellody and John were breaking the funds apart was very, very angst-ridden. Calvert was not happy that Ariel was leaving, so nothing about the departure was easy. For Mellody, the anxiety manifested physically, and she couldn't eat. The only thing she could get down each day was a Mrs. Fields mandarin orange muffin. She was so overwhelmed because she felt like the entire future of Ariel was in jeopardy solely because of her suggestion. By the end of the summer, as the deal progressed toward closing, Mellody was down to a mere 90 pounds.

But Ariel successfully completed the deal, and much like other key strategies Mellody has outlined and executed throughout her career, it proved to be exactly the right path. While the joint board had agreed that Ariel would take over $400M in assets, by the time the dust settled, $100M in funds went with Calvert. Because Ariel brought over only $300M in assets, $100M less than planned, their original payment of $4M was reduced to $3M.

"The moment the companies separated," Mellody reflected, "was the moment I went from being an employee of the company to truly being a partner, as its future was so much under my vision and direction." Fast forward to today, and Ariel has billions of dollars under management, and Mellody has ascended to the role of president of the company. She put her job and career on the line to get the deal that transformed the company and Mellody's position within it.

KEY POINT IN THIS DEAL:

- Many of the best startup founders are relatively inexperienced business people in their 20s. Their lack of experience, the fact that they're not jaded by a history of hearing "no," and the reality that they have little to lose all combine to create a strong position from which they can present bold ideas. The 20- and 30-somethings in your organization are likely to have the unbridled optimism and ambition to do transformative deals.

JOI ITO

MOVIE ACCOUNTING IS A LOT LIKE A BOX OF CHOCOLATES MONKEY POINTS

I first met Joi Ito about 15 years ago, when we were both invited to an exclusive annual event called the Sony Open Forum. At the time, I was the chief strategy officer for RealNetworks, and I was working closely with Sony. Joi was a Japanese entrepreneur who already had a few successful businesses under his belt, and he was there to advise Sony as well.

Since then, Joi and I have become friends and see each other annually at various technology events. Joi's star has continued to rise. For the last several years, he has been the Director of the MIT Media Lab, one of the most coveted technical positions in the country, and he serves on the boards of directors of both the Sony Corporation and the *New York Times*.

With his extensive experience in international business, technology, and entertainment, Joi shared a few interesting stories with me regarding deals he was instrumental in. One that caught my attention adds to the overall scope of the deals covered in this book. It concerns the time Joi was hired as an assistant to the executive producer of a Hollywood film that was being financed by a Japanese conglomerate. The deal dates back to the early 90s, though the lessons learned are relevant today.

The Japanese conglomerate NHK was one of the largest broadcasters in the world and wanted to get into the production of Hollywood movies. NHK forged a partnership with Thom Mount, a hot, young Hollywood producer of his time who had been named president of Universal Pictures when he was just 26. NHK struck a ten-movie deal with Thom under a new entity called Media International Corporation. The first of the ten films was called *Indian Runner*, and Sean Penn was hired to direct it.

Shortly after the film went into production, the NHK executive who had orchestrated the deal was relocated to a different part of the company, and with that, his influence and authority were taken away. Joi told me that in Japanese companies, this is a common strategy for taking people out of power. With the loss of that champion from NHK, support for the ten-movie deal quickly fizzled, and nobody at NHK was willing to work on *Indian Runner*. However, Thom moved forward with the film, assuming NHK would stand behind the deal and honor their financial obligations.

To ensure financial support for his film, Thom called Jack Valenti, then the head of the Motion Picture Association of America (MPAA). Thom asked Jack to get the U.S. State Department involved to guarantee that NHK would meet their obligations. The MPAA put a call into NHK, reminding them of their commitment and strongly suggesting, "You don't screw Hollywood." This caused quite a stir.

Joi's mother, who had worked as an executive in American and Japanese companies, was often called in to help resolve international disputes, and NHK decided to pull her into this conflict. She led the negotiations between Thom and NFK, eventually haggling to the point where NHK would be responsible only for *Indian Runner*, which was already in pre-production and accruing expenses. The budget for the film was roughly $15M.

Thom was frustrated and concerned that NHK would prove difficult to work with. He needed a Japanese liaison who could operate as an intermediary between himself and NHK. Joi's mother immediately thought of her son as someone who understood the two cultures and would be respected by both sides. She introduced him to Thom, who hired Joi as his assistant.

Joi was in an interesting position. NHK assumed he would be more on their side because he was Japanese. Thom assumed Joi would be more on his side because Thom was his boss and paying his salary. On balance, this worked out well, because each side perceived that Joi was doing right by them. Each side thought he favored them a bit more, which allowed them to trust Joi and feel good about his role. This is the key "soul" point in this deal: If each side feels you are slightly more aligned with *them* even though you have an equal stake in both sides' success, a deal can progress more smoothly, and much can be accomplished.

Joi learned a lot about film, finance, and international relations through the process of working on *Indian Runner*. Sean Penn had negotiated final cut privilege when he agreed to come on as director, which meant he would make all final decisions on what was and was not in the movie and how the movie would be released.

One of the first negotiations that tested Joi in this role was when NHK began asking for final cut. Joi, who was getting a quick education on these issues, told NHK that although they were financing the film, they did not have final cut. This had been reserved for Sean Penn.

Joi also learned about completion bonds, a financial instrument that ensures that the funds a film's various investors have agreed to provide are in fact available to complete it. The bond company assigns an expert to oversee the production costs of the film to make sure it doesn't lose money. For this film, Sam "The Legend" Goldrich was hired to oversee production. (Sam made a name for himself as Woody Allen's accountant.) He would come to the set, read the script, review the production plan, and determine whether the film was on a path to stay on budget.

While Sean Penn had final cut, Sam had the right to literally cut pages out of the script to make sure the film would not go over budget. Cutting pages is a delicate process, but Sam "The Legend" had a reputation for being able to do this in a way that didn't compromise the quality of the end product.

Joi was in the middle again. He had been in the middle between NHK and Thom Mount, and now he was in the middle between Sam "The Legend" and Sean Penn. In this intermediary role, Joi was once again always fair and balanced. Sean and Sam each believed Joi "had their back," and this helped the film move through production. This was a great training ground for Joi, who has always been an adept and quick learner. He learned that there is a lot to learn on a movie set—far more than most people realize.

During the filming of *Indian Summer*, Joi was given a glimpse into Hollywood accounting. He learned about "monkey points," for example. In Hollywood, the term "monkey points" is used when an actor is offered a percentage (points) of the profit from the film rather than a percentage (points) of its gross revenue. The problem with monkey points is that studios sometimes burden films with so many expenses that even the most successful do not show a profit.

An illustrative story about monkey points comes from the film *Forrest Gump*, which grossed over $600M. (At the time, it was the third highest-grossing movie ever.) The author of the book on which the movie was based was granted monkey points for the project instead of gross points. Even though he was entitled to 3% of the net profit, he only made $350K. Had the author been granted gross points and not monkey points, he would have made $18M. The studio claimed the film was unprofitable. (Tom Hanks earned a whopping $31M for his efforts.)

Another fascinating element of Hollywood accounting with which Joi became very familiar during the filming of *Indian Summer* was cash flow.

Joi said that while filming in Omaha, Nebraska, each day, problems arose that could best be resolved with cash. For example, the production team would be all set to shoot a scene and find out that the air conditioner in the local building they were using made too much noise. Rather than waiting hours for the air conditioner to go off, which would cost a fortune in delays, the line producer would approach the owner of the building and offer him several hundred bucks to turn it off. This might not seem like a lot of money, but on big productions, tens of thousands of dollars in cash can be paid out in just a few days. Typically, there is little documentation of exactly where the cash is going.

It's up to the studio to provide a full balance sheet for all expenses associated with a film. In addition to cash expenses, all marketing and production costs—literally anything they can think of—is put against the revenue of the film. This is how a film like *Forrest Gump*, which grossed over $600M, can be determined a "loss." Lesson learned in Hollywood: Watch your back, and don't get caught being a monkey.

KEY POINTS IN THIS DEAL:

- If you're in the middle of two sides, try to help them come together by persuading each of them you're a little more on *their* side. This puts you in a great position to close the gap, especially if you remain fair.

- Understand the details of how deals are done in a given industry so that you don't get burned by structures that disadvantage one side over the other.

APPLE, MEET STANFORD.
STANFORD, MEET APPLE.

My first job out of college was working for Apple at their head-quarters in Cupertino, California as part of their Macintosh development team. It was an awesome first job. I fell in love with Macintosh as soon as it was released, and could viscerally feel the impending impact it was going to have on personal computing. Getting that first job at Apple was not a choice; it was destiny.

Working at Apple in the early days of Macintosh was amazing. Everyone in the company believed they were a part of something that was going to change the world. We worked well into the evenings and sometimes pulled all-nighters. It was very reminiscent of college culture. (Note: I specifically refer to the machine as Macintosh, never "The Macintosh." Steve hated the article; he thought it belittled the importance of Macintosh.

At the time, the Apple II was still the main computer of the company. Consequentially, there was rivalry and tension between the Macintosh division and other company divisions, such as the Apple II's. Steve Jobs had taken to the Macintosh division, and as such, he lavished us with his attention and creative energy. (Note: As an entry-level software engineer, I had little to no interaction with Steve; that came much later.) Inspirational posters that embodied Steve's vision lined the walls. One I specifically remember was: The Journey Is the Reward.

The Macintosh group at Apple recognized that there needed to be dozens—if not hundreds—of software applications available for Macintosh to compete with the IBM PC, which launched at around the same time as Macintosh. When Macintosh was first released in January 1984, developer tools weren't even available for it, so the only software that shipped were titles by Apple such as MacWrite and MacPaint.

Apple took a couple of steps to fix this dearth of software titles. First, they developed an engineer-friendly compiler (geek speak for a tool that writes software apps) so that third parties had the tools to build applications for Macintosh. In addition, they set up a formal group called "Evangelism" whose job was to meet with companies and engineers who were developing for the IBM PC and convince them to develop their products for Macintosh as well.

When I was an undergraduate upperclassman at UCLA, I worked as a teaching assistant for some of the computer science professors. This was an awesome job. I sat in on lectures, helped the professors grade papers, and held office hours during which I basically tutored students. The job paid pretty well, and more important, I was given access to the suite of offices used by the computer science professors.

It's important to mention the state of computing back in 1982, when I was a TA. Paper Punch Cards (look it up on Wikipedia :-)) had finally been outdated as primary computer programming. Instead, we had what were known as "dumb terminals" that gave you access to a mainframe computer housed deep within UCLA's Boelter Hall (known as the birthplace of the Internet).

Only about 20 dumb terminals were available in the student lab. As a student, you had to sign up to get your two hours a day at one, and there, you could write your code in what are now far outdated programming languages: Cobalt, Fortran, Pascal, as well as the new-to-the-scene, simply-titled "C." In those two hours a day, you had to get your code typed in, tested, debugged, and working.

Because I was a TA, I was granted 24/7 access to the suite where all of the professors had offices equipped with dedicated dumb terminals. This meant I could code anytime, day or night, without having to sign up for the public lab or worry about getting only two hours a day.

When I reached Apple and was programming away as an entry-level engineer, writing code at all hours of the day and night, I thought to myself, "What Apple really needs is a 'How to Program for Macintosh' class at Stanford." Stanford had long been one of the top schools in the country, especially for computer science. What better way to gain an army of Macintosh-programming enthusiasts than to teach eager, enterprising Stanford students?

But there was one problem: I would not be able to teach the class myself. I was not educated as a teacher and had never actually taught a class (minus a few working sessions as a TA). Stanford also prided itself on having professors with doctoral degrees, and I did not have one. In addition, Stanford did not have a Macintosh lab, and the university was too far from Apple's Cupertino headquarters for students to travel there. Rather than allow this last limitation to be a barrier, however, I decided to use it as an opportunity.

Despite my lack of teaching credentials, I went ahead and put together a syllabus for teaching programming for the Macintosh. I went to my boss at Apple and my boss' boss and so on, and I pitched the idea of my teaching the class at Stanford. It wouldn't cost Apple any money. All Apple had to do was to provide 20 Macintosh Plus computers and about four or five laser printers for use in a dedicated lab.

The senior management at Apple received the proposal extremely well. Then, I needed to close the deal with Stanford. Through some old friends from the school, I found out who the chairman of the Computer Science Department was. A few of these friends who were working in the department helped arrange a meeting with the chairman simply by saying Apple had a proposal for them.

I met with the chairman and laid out the plan: Stanford would receive a state of the art Macintosh computer lab *gratis*, and I would teach an upper division class. Again, this was a real stretch given I had never taught and had no degrees to back me up. But I put forth the proposal anyway, and to my surprise, the department accepted it on the spot.

The next semester, I started teaching Computer Science 193C: Programming for the Macintosh to upperclassmen. I taught the class for two semesters until I moved back to Los Angeles to start my first company, After Hours Software.

Postscript: Computer Science 193C is still taught at Stanford to this day. It has produced a few decades' worth of talented programmers who have gone on to develop some of the most sophisticated software for Macintosh and Apple. This deal got done because it provided obvious benefits to each side and literally no downside other than my lack of professional credentials. Fortunately, this didn't stop the deal from being done.

KEY POINT IN THIS DEAL:

- Unbridled enthusiasm and passion can sometimes overcome bureaucratic rules about what an organization can and cannot do. Appeal to a missing piece of a stodgy organization's operations to help them overcome their inertia.

THE SOUL OF THIS BOOK

P art of the struggle of writing this book and trying to help you be a better deal maker is my core thesis: You cannot teach someone how to be a great deal maker by giving them a series of steps to follow. However, the overriding themes presented in this book and the organization of its chapters should go a long way toward helping you navigate future deals.

Becoming a great deal maker takes a lot of experience, as I hope you've gleaned from this book. It's about learning to trust your gut as you feel your way through *The Soul of a Deal*, and keeping an open and creative mind as deals evolve.

Don't set yourself up for disappointment by assuming all deals should be closed. Some deals just don't work out. Identifying as early as possible when deals are not going to work out is just as important closing the deals that do.

In the end, deal making is about soul. Your soul. It's about listening to that inner voice that guides you on what to do, where to go, and when to raise complex issues. This dictates what you are willing to accept in a deal and when the other side crosses the line. Listen to your inner soul, your very being. This is the message of this book above all else. I wish you the best of luck in letting your soul guide you through the deals that come to you throughout your career.

ACKNOWLEDGEMENTS

F irst, I would like to thank each of the people I interviewed for *The Soul of a Deal*. Not only because this book would quite literally not have been possible without them, but also because they did much more than simply give me interviews. They read drafts of chapters (in some cases, the entire manuscript) and generously offered up additional insight into their stories and feedback on my telling of others'. I'm so grateful to each of them for investing in me and this book their most valuable asset—time. I won't list their names here, but these men and women are given their well deserved recognition on the cover of this book as well as in its table of contents and chapter headings.

I also had help from a great group of professionals that helped with everything from proofreading to organization, layout, and self-publishing, including Kim Hall, Kelly McNamara, Marites Seitz, and Brooke White.

In addition, I would like to thank the following people for taking time out of their busy schedules to read this book and provide me with invaluable feedback: Alan Citron, Professor Emeritus Lee Cooper, Kevin Efrusy, Csaba Konkley, Dan Lyons, Vince Thompson, and Mike Wolpert.

Made in the USA
San Bernardino, CA
29 November 2018